DA SILVANO COOKBOOK

DA SILVANO

COOKBOOK

SIMPLE SECRETS FROM NEW YORK'S

FAVORITE ITALIAN RESTAURANT

SILVANO MARCHETTO

WITH ANDREW FRIEDMAN
AND SCOTT HAAS

FOREWORD BY NICK TOSCHES

PHOTOGRAPHS BY ROBERT DiScalfani

BLOOMSBURY

Published by Bloomsbury, New York and London
Distributed to the trade by St. Martin's Press

Library of Congress Cataloging-in-Publication Data
Marchetto, Silvano, 1946-
    Da Silvano cookbook: simple secrets from New York's favorite Italian restaurant/
  Silvano Marchetto; foreword by Nick Tosches; photographs by Robert DiScalfani.
      p. cm.
    ISBN 1-58234-117-6
    1. Cookery, Italian. 2. Da Silvano (Restaurant) I. Title.

    TX723 .M327 2001
    641.5945—dc21

                                                                                2001035864

First U.S. Edition

10 9 8 7 6 5 4 3 2 1

Design by Vertigo Design, NYC
Printed and bound by C & C Offset Printing Co., Ltd., Hong Kong

for DAWN AND LeyLa

acknowledgements

MY DEEPEST THANKS GOES TO...

Karen Rinaldi, who first believed in the book.

Colin Dickerman, for shepherding it to completion.

Nick Tosches, my first customer of each and every day, for his wonderful foreword.

Andrew Wylie, my agent, who put the whole thing together.

Andrew Friedman, for his last-minute help.

Segundo "Luigi" S. Naula and Alessandro Bandini, for making my restaurant run smoothly.

Michael J. Belardo, for his help in selecting the wines.

Graydon Carter, for his special support of the project.

And to my customers at Da Silvano. This is really for all of you.

Da SILVANO

Cucina Toscana

CONTENTS

from where I sit, at table thirty

(DON'T EVEN THINK OF TRYING TO SIT HERE)

nick tosches

Where do I begin? These are words by which no writer should ever expose himself in print, even though they be deeply and forever embedded in the cerebral crenulations by which his trade may be detected, identified, defined. Yet, here, this question is the beginning, the only beginning; and neither the deft, cheap glibness of a journeyman-hack, such as myself, or the magisterial Quintilian eloquence of a master of poetry and of prose, such as myself, can vanquish it, evade it, or veil it. For the plain truth is that there is no known beginning, not as far as Silvano and I can recall. We have known one another a good and long time, but neither of us can remember when and how we met.

Silvano Marchetto was born, in 1946, in northern Italy, in Trento, where his father, a career military officer, was then stationed. As his family moved to Florence in 1948, Silvano has no memory of Trento but only of Florence. Aside from his paternal grandfather, who was a baker in Treviso and whom he never met, there was no more culinary influence in his background than is to be found in the kitchen of any family. His father, he says, was a good cook. As for his mother, he uses the same kind phrase by which I recollect my own mother's cooking: "She tried." None the less, to speak of Silvano's youth and early manhood—that is to say, of those parts of which can be politely spoken—is to speak of food. Some may know the ancient town of Fiesole, upon a hill about three miles northeast of the heart of Florence, as a source from which, according to legend, the stone that built Florence was quarried. Others may know Fiesole from the *Commedia*, where Dante turns to it in both the *Inferno* and the *Paradiso*. Silvano knows it as the place where he worked as a broiler-cook, at the Ristorante Raspanti.

Kitchen work and waitering, in and around Florence; and, in the last of his teenage years, when he was seventeen to nineteen, in Paris. He arrived in New York in the fall of 1968. He was a waiter at the Portofino restaurant, on Thompson Street in Greenwich Village; a waiter at the Derby steak house nearby on MacDougal Street—two now-vanished landmarks of the days when the Village was the Village.

One of the most evocative remembrances of those vanished Village days was Bimbo's, at 260 Sixth Avenue, between Bleecker and Houston streets. It was a small semi-private eating establishment, a joint whose patrons were mostly gentlemen of a darkly taciturn sort. After Bimbo passed away, Silvano took over the place, on May 1, 1975. He called it Da Silvano. While *di* is the possessive singular in Italian—Silvano's restaurant would be il ristorante *di* Silvano—and while the preposition *da* means from, it can also be used in referring to a destination that is defined by the name or profession of a person. Thus, instead of *vado al ristorante di Silvano*—meaning, I'm going to Silvano's restaurant—the simpler *vado da Silvano*, meaning, I'm going to Silvano's.

Like Bimbo's before it, Silvano's place was originally only the room one now enters upon arrival. It was in 1982 that he acquired the space next door, broke through the wall, and expanded the joint to its present size. Da Silvano was here to stay. I will tell you why, though the recipes in this book will illuminate this with far greater light. First, however, I should like to offer illumination of another sort. For there is no recipe for Silvano himself; and, regarding him, I find the words of William Painter, uttered centuries ago, to be of pertinence: "I thinke dame Nature her selfe hath broken the mould."

Images, occurrences flow through my mind. I remember Silvano skulking through the door in an oversized dark coat—the sort that thieves refer to as boosting coats—looking warily around, then approaching me, reaching into his pocket, his eyes wide with hushed excitement, as if he were about to withdraw from that pocket something either of unimaginable value or of sinfulness most forbidden and illicit. Then he revealed it to me: a stillborn piglet, barely bigger than the palm of his hand. "I cook it now. We eat it," he enthused. As my companion watched Silvano's eager departure to the kitchen then looked at me with repulsion, I recalled aloud with relish the rows of such delicacies, some still in placentae, displayed outdoors at the *salumeria* in Voghera.

Of course, many who would eagerly eat the hormone-poisoned flesh of a cruelly murdered cow would, like my companion, turn away from such a rare and savorous luxury. And, to be truthful, whenever he roasts a lamb, then cuts off the head and cleaves this *capozella* in twain for us to share—brimming with tender brain-meat and sparse with the morsels of delicious jowl-flesh called *gota*—we both always shy away from spooning out and eating the eyeballs, which my grandfather told me again and again were the very best part. But, eyeballs or no eyeballs, in the end, one can only truly experience the richness of what Silvano offers if one is willing to have faith in his love for the finest food, and in his heartfelt dedication to, and pride in, fulfilling that love.

Working with only the highest quality and freshest ingredients, he is ever experimenting with new sorceries. Unlike those pervasive restaurateurs whose confections are but sculptural variations on the same cloying and tiresome *nouvelle* shucking and jiving, Silvano seeks not new looks or frills but rather new subtleties of taste. With a perceptive awareness of the essence of every ingredient, he strives for, and achieves, the elusive and delicate marriage of the simple and the sublime.

If the grain that we call spelt—known in Italy as *spelta*, from that same late Latin word, and as *farro*, from the older Latin word *far*—was good enough to keep the ancient Roman troops strong, it is good enough, figures Silvano, to serve as the base of one of his best soups. His other soups are also as salubrious and magnificently straightforward, from his Tuscan specialty, *ribollita*, to my own favorite, a garlic soup more potent than the pharmacopoeia of the ages. This is Silvano's brilliance: to know that these things are as important as the quail eggs on polenta with shaved white truffles. Or the half-onion and caviar.

By way of overture to a symphony of general discontent with so-called civilization as we know it I once wrote:

"I sit, and I ponder the onion that has been placed before me. For this particular onion bespeaks more than the whole of the Uffizi the true nature of Italian creativity, more than the whole of Machiavelli the true nature of Tuscan cunning.

"It is, to be precise, not even an onion, but merely half an onion. Ah, but it is half a Walla Walla onion—this fact is flaunted—roasted and topped with a smidgen of caviar. The price is thirty-five dollars. As the cost of a single, one-

pound Walla Walla onion is about a dollar, and the cost of beluga caviar well under twenty-five dollars an ounce, this half an onion and its smidgen must be worth about five or six bucks. Mysticized into a rare and precious delicacy by my friend, it is a very popular item: whenever the caviar runs out, the fifty-cent half onion is served at a price of ten dollars."

Silvano then proceeded to raise the price of the half-onion and caviar by half a buck. I then proceeded to eat more of them.

This was not long before the time I walked in for lunch as he sat there browsing a magazine feature about him and his restaurant, his eyes coming upon the line, "Author Nick Tosches, a daily lunch visitor who treats the restaurant as his home office, even having his pay checks and FedExes sent there, jokes, 'Silvano is multilingually unintelligible.'" Some days later, before I was leaving for two months on a remote Sicilian island, he told me he planned to visit me—his keys are always mine to use, mine are always his—and he asked me how to get there. I wrote down instructions in Italian, very detailed, down to the note that, of the two doors that shared the same address, mine was *la porta alla sinistra*, the door to the

left. But there was a typographical error: I had written *sinestra* for *sinistra*. He seemed to study the directions with unduly absorbed scrutiny. Then, finally, he burst forth, gloating: "Look at this! Sin—ay—stra!" he declaimed derisively. "Humph! The word is sin—ee—stra, not sin—ay—stra! Humph! Is unintelligible!"

The author of a profile of me once wrote: "Choosing a place to meet Nick Tosches for lunch in New York is a foregone conclusion. Every day he eats at the same table at the same restaurant, Da Silvano." It was at this same table at this same restaurant, Da Silvano, that I was interviewed by a writer from *Time* magazine who wanted my thoughts on Vincent Gigante, who was then on trial. I gave him my thoughts, and the reporter, who described me as "a novelist who sits in Da Silvano every day, same window table," went on to write: "'The federal witness-protection program is welfare for rats,' Nick Tosches says, referring to the low-life grunts who have testified, 'and if they convict Gigante through these nefarious means, it's a death knell for this neighborhood. You used to be able to leave your doors and windows open around here. For years Gigante has been a benevolent presence, and I'd rather have him as a neighbor than any cop in the Sixth Precinct.'" As I said before, the old Village no longer exists; and most of the cops there no longer even live in or know the neighborhood. I doubt that my words endeared me to them.

And, of course, it was as I was approaching Da Silvano that two squad cars and a paddy wagon converged on me. "I don't think he's going to be able to make it tonight," Silvano discreetly and without further details told my guest when she arrived.

In the end, this all comes together towards delving the secret of Silvano's success. For one thing, the main thing, there is the food. His menu and his daily specials are a perfect balance of the constant and the constantly changing. It was Edward Dahlberg who said, "Originality is but high-born stealth," a truth that Silvano is the first to acknowledge. His *panna cotta*, which is the best I have ever tasted anywhere in the world, is, he freely admits, derived from a recipe he stealthily drew forth from a chef at a restaurant in the vicinity of Lake Como. Once, when I returned from Paris having encountered a remarkable *tartar tonique* of chilled herbs and diced vegetables, we together deduced triumphantly that the substance that held it together was mashed avocado.

Silvano does not hesitate to name what he believes to be the best restaurant in Florence: Da I'Frasca sull'Ambra. But asked if his is the best Italian restaurant in New York, he pauses. "One of the best," he says. Then, after some deliberation, neither of us can come up with a better one. For southern Italian food, made and served as it should be, there is Rao's, in East Harlem. But for food whose soul is both timeless as the ancient grain of imperium and as new as the imagination's endless pullulations, there is only one joint I know, only one joint to which I go. As my buddy Oliver Ray put it as we sat together at lunch, "This is where I first discovered food that transformed eating into a consciousness-altering experience."

And, to me, a part of the magic, a part of the secret of Da Silvano, has something to do with the vanished old days. For, as fashionable and popular as his place has become, Silvano remains a stand-up guy, and he has not given priority to celebrity poseurs and their ways over the neighborhood characters and their ways. I have shown up there on a particularly bad day wearing sweatpants, slippers, and a bathrobe, and was treated with the same dignity, and with greater friendliness, than were the regal dame and her retinue at the table across from me.

Enough of tale and praise. They say that if you can read, you can cook. And so it is that you now hold the *chiave d'oro*, the key of gold, that alone truly unlocks the secret.

INtRODUCtION

My restaurant, Da Silvano, has been going strong for more than twenty-five years and yet I've never written a cookbook. Why? To tell you the truth, I've been too busy. The restaurant is my life. I'm there every morning, looking after the place, making sure all the food that shows up from our purveyors is as good as it should be, and getting the dining room ready for my first guests of the day, beginning with the great writer Nick Tosches, who did a better job telling you about me and my restaurant in this book's foreword than I ever could. Well, maybe I could do a better job in Italian. But in English? No way.

But people have been asking me for a book for years. They want to know how much garlic goes in the garlic soup, or how to make gnocchi so light, or what exactly puntarelle is. They want to know how I got the idea for the famous *Vulcano Silvano* or what the recipe is for my *Panna Cotta*. We're not known for desserts at Da Silvano, but that *Panna Cotta!* Everybody wants to know how to make it. But I've never told. Not until now.

Well, here they are—all the answers to all the questions. I hope nobody's disappointed, because there aren't any big surprises here. Nothing too shocking or revolutionary. You're not going to find me putting cheese in my fish dishes (well, OK, I do it in one dish), or overcooking pasta rather than making it al dente, or making *Pappa al Pomodoro*, a tomato-and-bread soup, with green and yellow tomatoes instead of juicy red ones.

I'm a pretty traditional guy, and I think that's what shows in my cooking. I'm very proud of my Italian heritage and of the food of my people. I love sharing that food with my customers and I've enjoyed writing this book because it allows me to share it with you, even if you've never been to Italy, or even to New York.

As you'll see, the secret to what we do at Da Silvano is paying careful attention to our ingredients and letting each one shine as much as possible. If I could give one piece of advice to anyone who wants to cook well, it would be to respect the food. This is especially true today, when so many cooks are trying to invent something new and exciting. To me, there's nothing more exciting than great ingredients prepared with respect and love. If I want to see something new, I'll go to the movies.

Enjoy this book, and if you find yourself in New York, make some time to drop by Da Silvano. We serve lunch well into the afternoon and dinner late into the evening, so there's really no excuse not to. You should come in and have a bowl of pasta and a glass of wine and see how special simple food can be.

Silvano Marchetto

NEW YORK CITY

APRIL 2001

DA SILVANO COOKBOOK

antipasti
APPETIZERS

When it comes to appetizers, my philosophy is "the simpler, the better." I don't just favor simple *recipes*; I think appetizers should be a simple *experience*—clean, fresh ingredients and not too many flavors on one plate.

My customers seem to agree. This chapter features our most popular appetizers. Many of them are small, hors d'oeuvre-type offerings like Crostini Toscani, Italian chopped chicken livers spread over toasted ciabatta; or a *Bruschetta* of diced tomatoes and basil. Others feature just one perfect thing, like *Sarde alla Griglia*, or grilled sardines; *Cozze alla Marinara*, or mussels cooked in white wine sauce; and *Puntarelle*, an Italian chicory that's crunchy, clean, and delicious.

I also like bold contrasts, and in a few dishes I have paired two primary and very complementary ingredients. Most of these are classic combinations, like *Rapini con Salsiccia*, which is broccoli di rapa with spicy

sausage, and *Fave con Pecorino*, a salad of fava beans and Pecorino Toscano cheese. But a few are of my own design, most notably the *Carpaccio di Coda Rospo e Melone Cantalope*, a monkfish and melon dish that was inspired by a trip to St. Tropez.

I've also included a number of salads including *Panzanella*, a bread salad; *Panzanella di Farro*, a variation on the bread salad made with spelt; *Barbabietole e Indivia*, a salad of beets and endive; and *Viareggina*, which features hearts of palm and avocado—a wonderful combination.

There are many more recipes in the pages to follow, but I'll tell you about them as we get to them. I think that a book, like a meal, should leave something to the imagination, and I'd like to surprise you a little along the way.

BRUSCHetta

The simplicity and flavors of bruschetta perfectly reflect the spirit of late summer, which is the best time to make and enjoy it because it depends on the best, freshest tomatoes for its success.

Notice how much flavor you get out of garlic just by rubbing it on the toasted bread—there's none of it in the finished dish, but you taste its essence in every bite.

serves 4

6 plum tomatoes, cut into ½-inch/1-cm cubes

10 fresh basil leaves

5 tablespoons extra virgin olive oil

Fine sea salt

Freshly ground black pepper

Small loaf crusty Tuscan bread, cut into 8 slices (½ inch/1 cm each)

1 clove garlic, peeled

Place the tomatoes in a ceramic or stainless steel mixing bowl. Tear the basil leaves into small pieces and add them. Drizzle the olive oil over the tomatoes and basil and season with salt and pepper. Gently mix the tomatoes, basil, and oil with a wooden spoon. Taste and adjust the seasoning if necessary. Set aside.

Toast the bread slices. Place the garlic on the tines of a fork and brush it once on the upward-facing side of the toast slices in a Z pattern.

Spoon some tomato-basil mixture on each slice, arrange the slices on a platter, and serve immediately.

WINE SUGGESTION: **Arneis "Blangé"–Ceretto**

NO TOMATOES?

For a variation on this dish, make a *fettunta* (oily slice) by brushing the garlic on each slice of bread in a Z pattern, toasting the slices, and drizzling them with olive oil.

crostini toscani

TOASTED CIABATTA WITH SAUTÉED CHICKEN LIVERS

Crostini are lightly toasted slices of bread topped with vegetables, meat, or a combination of the two. At Da Silvano, we serve crostini with chicken livers that have been sautéed with onions, wine, capers, and anchovies, then cut up just until they are spreadable.

It's best to use day-old ciabatta, a small, thin-crusted bread—the juice will soak in and soften it to create the perfect texture.

SERVES 4

2 tablespoons olive oil

½ medium red onion, roughly chopped

1 pound/450g chicken livers, membranes removed

1 teaspoon small capers, drained but not rinsed (see Note)

4 anchovy fillets

½ cup/120 ml dry white wine

1 loaf ciabatta, cut into 8 to 10 slices (½ inch/1 cm each), lightly toasted

1 tablespoon minced flat-leaf parsley

Warm the olive oil in a sauté pan wide enough to hold the livers in a single layer over medium heat. Add the onions and cook until lightly colored, about 4 minutes. Add the chicken livers and brown them on all sides, cooking until medium-rare, about 5 minutes. Add the capers and anchovies. Cook, stirring to prevent scorching, for 5 minutes. Add the wine and cook until reduced but not dry, 2 to 3 minutes.

Pour the contents of the skillet into a fine-mesh strainer set over a bowl. Reserve the juice to add some of it to the livers if they are too dry.

Turn the onions, livers, capers, and anchovies out onto a clean, dry cutting board and chop roughly until they are well incorporated and the mixture is spreadable. If it appears too dry, spoon some reserved cooking liquid over it and chop again. Transfer the mixture to a small bowl.

Spread some chopped liver on each slice of toast. Sprinkle some chopped parsley over each one. Serve at room temperature.

NOTE: Don't use salt-packed capers; they're much too salty, especially since I don't believe in rinsing capers before using them. Purchase those stored in brine.

WINE SUGGESTION: **Chianti Classico "Scassino"–Terrabianca**

fagioli con pancetta e rucola

BEANS WITH PANCETTA AND RUCOLA

White Spanish beans—also referred to as butter beans—are wonderful receivers of flavor. Cooked with radicchio and tossed with browned pancetta, they really come alive. The key to this recipe is the red wine vinegar—you add only a splash, but it gives the entire dish an acidic bite and cuts the fattiness of the pancetta.

serves 4

1 pound/450g (about 1 cup) dried white Spanish beans

Fine sea salt

Freshly ground black pepper

1 small head of radicchio (about 8 oz/225g), tough core removed and separated into leaves

1 small red onion, quartered (see Note)

2 ounces/55g rucola (about 1¼ cups loosely packed), coarsely chopped (see Note)

8 ounces/225g thinly sliced pancetta, cut into thin strips (see Note)

1 tablespoon red wine vinegar

Soak the beans overnight in enough cold water to cover. Drain.

Place the beans in a pot and cover them by 2 inches/5 cm with cold water. Season with salt and pepper. Add the onion and radicchio and bring to a boil over high heat. Lower the heat and simmer until the beans are tender and cooked through, about 1 hour.

About 10 minutes before the beans are done, place the pancetta in a sauté pan and cook, stirring, over medium-high heat until the pancetta is nicely browned and some fat has rendered, 4 to 5 minutes.

When the beans are done, drain them in a colander. Remove and discard the onion and transfer the beans to the pan with the pancetta. Cook for 1 to 2 minutes over low heat, tossing to combine the flavors.

Transfer the pancetta-bean mixture to a large platter, drizzle with a splash of red wine vinegar, and top with the rucola. Serve at once.

NOTES: When quartering onions that will need to be removed from a recipe, as here, be sure to leave the root end of each onion intact so that the layers don't separate.

Rucola is a peppery green that is often called "arugula" in the United States. But, as with broccoli rabe, which I call by the Italian broccoli di rapa, I prefer to use the Italian name, rucola.

Pancetta is, basically, cured bacon, which comes from the belly of the pig. It is an Italian staple and is available from many specialty and gourmet shops.

WINE SUGGESTION: **Mondaccione–Coppo**

fave con pecorino

FAVA BEANS AND PECORINO TOSCANO

In Tuscany, fava beans and Pecorino Toscano cheese are a classic springtime combination because that's when the beans come into season. There, we don't serve them in a salad—instead we sit, preferably outside, each person peeling his own beans and cutting pieces of cheese from a large wedge.

At Da Silvano, I serve *Fave con Pecorino* whenever I can get my hands on fresh beans, not just the spring. (In January for example, I get them from California.) Peeling fava beans takes a lot of time, but is well worth it.

SERVES 4

2 pounds/900g fava beans, peeled (see Note)

4 ounces/110g Pecorino Toscano, sliced into ½-inch/1-cm-long, matchstick-thick segments

¼ cup/55ml olive oil

Fine sea salt

Freshly ground black pepper

2 leaves radicchio, sliced very thin

Place the fava beans and pecorino in a small mixing bowl. Drizzle the olive oil over the top and season with salt and pepper. Toss very gently just to combine the flavors and being careful not to break the beans or crush the cheese.

Mound a quarter of the beans and cheese in the center of each of 4 salad plates. Top each serving with a few slivers of radicchio.

NOTE: Peeling fava beans requires two steps: First, carefully remove the tough outer pod. (If you like, you can run a paring knife along the seam, but be careful not to push in too far or you'll cut the bean.) Then, carefully remove the skin that envelops each individual bean. One pound/450g of fava beans in the pod yields about ½ cup/110g of beans.

WINE SUGGESTION: **Chianti Classico–*Rocca delle Macie***

A More Complex Version

For a variation on this recipe, do as my friends at Da I'Frasca of Montevarchi do: For each serving, top ¼ cup/55g fava beans with 2 tablespoons cooked and cooled cannellini beans, drizzle with the olive oil, *then* top with Pecorino Toscano and a few shavings of white or black truffle.

carpaccio

They say that carpaccio (and the bellini, too) was invented by Mr. Cipriani at Harry's Bar in Venice. In New York today, there are all kinds of carpaccio, made with fish, duck, and even fruit. My way is easier than all the others, and even simpler than Mr. Cipriani's, who puts mayonnaise on his.

Because this recipe is so simple, every ingredient counts—use the best beef, the freshest lemon and rucola, and the finest Parmigiano-Reggiano. To keep the meat as cold as possible, put the plates in the refrigerator for a few minutes before preparing this dish.

SERVES 4

2 cups/110g roughly chopped rucola

4 tablespoons olive oil

Juice of ½ lemon

Fine sea salt

Freshly ground black pepper

¾ pound/340g eye round beef, cleaned and sliced paper-thin by your butcher, each slice kept refrigerated between sheets of wax paper (see Note)

4 ounces/110g Parmigiano-Reggiano, shaved into shards with a vegetable peeler

In a ceramic or stainless steel mixing bowl, toss the rucola with 3 tablespoons of the olive oil and the lemon juice and season to taste with salt and pepper.

Just before serving, lay overlapping slices of beef on each of 4 dinner plates to cover the surface in as even a layer as possible. Drizzle with the remaining 1 tablespoon olive oil and season lightly with salt and pepper.

Mound equal amounts of rucola on top of the beef in the center of each plate. Top the rucola with cheese shards, grind some black pepper over each plate, and serve immediately.

NOTE: To cut the beef yourself, place it in the freezer for a few minutes to firm it up, which will facilitate slicing. Use a slicing machine, or a very sharp chef's knife, keeping it as steady as possible to cut thin slices.

WINE SUGGESTION: **Chianti Classico–Fonterutoli**

segato di carciofi

When I tell new customers that the artichokes in this dish are raw, many of them can't believe it. But baby artichokes are so tender that this is the best way to enjoy all of their natural flavor. Even the choke is young enough that it can be eaten with no problem. In this recipe, the artichokes are tossed with olive oil and salt, then served under a little teepee of parmesan cheese for a beautiful presentation. You can also grate the cheese and toss it with the sliced artichokes if that seems more appealing to you.

SERVES 4

½ lemon

12 baby artichokes

Fine sea salt

2 tablespoons olive oil

12 paper-thin slices Parmigiano-Reggiano (about 3 inches by 4 inches/7.5 cm by 10 cm)

Freshly ground black pepper

Fill a stainless steel or ceramic bowl large enough to hold the artichokes with cold water. Squeeze the juice of the lemon into the bowl.

Clean and trim the artichokes by cutting off the stems and snapping back and removing all tough outer leaves. As each one is prepared, place the artichokes in the bowl with the lemon water to keep them from discoloring.

One by one, remove the artichokes from the lemon water. Slice each artichoke lengthwise as thin as possible, pat the slices dry with a paper towel, and collect them in a dry bowl. Season to taste with salt and drizzle with the olive oil. Toss gently.

Evenly divide the sliced artichokes and form into small mounds in the center of 4 salad plates. Form a tent of 3 slices of cheese over each mound. Grind some pepper over each plate and serve.

WINE SUGGESTION: **Greco di Tufo**

mamme

Whenever I prepare this recipe, I think of the Mercato Centrale in Florence. A lot of the farmers there sell artichokes, and they all call out to the shoppers, "*Mamme! Mamme!*", meaning theirs are the biggest, the most beautiful, the best.

This is my favorite way to serve artichokes. The beautiful presentation will surprise everyone and make the artichokes seem new and exciting.

SERVES 4

1 lemon, halved

4 large artichokes

Fine sea salt

¼ to ½ cup/55 to 110ml Vinaigrette Modo Mio (page 186)

1 tablespoon minced flat-leaf parsley

1 lemon, cut into thin slices

Fill a ceramic or stainless steel bowl large enough to hold the artichokes with cold water. Squeeze the juice of the 2 lemon halves into the water.

Cut the stems off the artichokes so that they can stand up on their ends. Set a paring knife at a slight angle to the base of 1 artichoke and turn the artichoke against the blade to trim the base of the artichoke and remove the small leaves. Use a chef's knife to trim the top 1 inch/2.5 cm off the artichoke, then use scissors to snip the sharp tips off the remaining leaves.

Place the artichoke in the lemon water and repeat with the remaining artichokes.

Bring a large pot of salted water to a boil.

Remove the artichokes from the lemon water, place them in the pot, and cook them at a gentle simmer until cooked through, about 35 minutes. Drain the artichokes and allow them to cool at room temperature.

Carefully spread the leaves out from the center of each artichoke. Gently remove the innermost cone of soft leaves. Use a small spoon (like an espresso spoon) to scrape off the choke (the heart's hairy covering).

Spoon 3 to 4 tablespoons of *vinaigrette* into the cavity of each artichoke, then tuck the cone of soft leaves into the cavity upside down.

Place 1 artichoke in the center of each of 4 bowls or salad plates, sprinkle parsley over each artichoke, and serve with the lemon slices alongside.

cozze aLLa marinara

MUSSELS IN WHITE WINE SAUCE

This dish reminds me of when my father used to take me to Marina di Massa in his army truck and we'd walk over the rocks along the shore, picking our own mussels, and then cook them on the beach for a delicious seaside lunch.

In Italy, you see garlic and white wine used to cook all kinds of fish dishes, but this is one of my favorites. You also see crushed red pepper in a lot of preparations because it adds flavor and heat in no time at all. I add the wine at the very end of the cooking process, so that it comes into contact with the mussels after they have opened and are ready to accept its flavor.

By the way, most Americans think of marinara sauce as being red, but the name actually means "from the sea." In Italy, a marinara sauce can be red or white.

If you like, serve the mussels with toasted country bread or bread slices that have been drizzled with olive oil and warmed on the grill or in a cast-iron pan.

SERVES 4

2 tablespoons olive oil

2 cloves garlic, smashed and peeled

4 pounds/1.8kg fresh mussels in their shells, cleaned and debearded, preferably Prince Edward Island mussels

Warm the olive oil in a casserole or pot large enough to hold the mussels over medium heat. Add the garlic and cook until it browns slightly, 2 to 3 minutes. Add the mussels. Add the red pepper. Cover the pot and cook until the mussels open, 3 to 5 minutes.

(If you don't have a large enough casserole, work in batches. Keep the first batch covered and warm in the serving bowl for the few minutes it takes to cook the second batch.)

¼ teaspoon crushed red pepper

Splash of dry white wine

12 cherry tomatoes, halved

20 caper berries

1 tablespoon minced flat-leaf parsley

Pour the wine over the mussels. It will evaporate almost immediately upon contact. Scatter the tomatoes and caper berries over the mussels.

Transfer the contents of the casserole to a large, deep, wide-mouthed bowl, discarding any that have not opened. Sprinkle the parsley over the mussels. Serve immediately, with another bowl alongside for guests to dispose of their empty shells.

WINE SUGGESTION: **Greco di Tufo–Mastroberardino**

INSALATA DI POLPO

My mother hated octopus, so when I first began to eat it, I did so out of spite. But now I do it out of love, because the flavor of this creature of the sea is like no other.

SERVES 4

Fine sea salt

2 octopuses (1 to 1½ lb/450g to 700g each)

2 medium Yukon Gold potatoes, scrubbed

2 lemons, halved

2 tablespoons olive oil

Freshly ground black pepper

¼ cup flat-leaf parsley leaves (loosely packed)

Fill a pot large enough to hold the octopuses with salted water and place over medium-high heat. Immediately add the octopuses and the potatoes and squeeze the juice of 2 lemon halves into the water. Bring the water to a boil. Cook for 30 to 40 minutes, or just until the potatoes are cooked through because—as some brilliant Italian discovered long ago—the potato and octopuses cook at the same rate. Check for doneness by inserting a small, thin-bladed knife into 1 potato. Be very careful not to overcook or the octopus will toughen. Remove the pot from the heat and let the octopuses and potatoes cool in the water for 30 to 40 minutes.

When cool, remove the potatoes from the water, cut them into ¼-inch/ 0.5-cm cubes, and transfer to a large bowl. Do not peel the potatoes. Remove the octopuses from the water and cut them into ½-inch/1-cm pieces. Add the octopus pieces to the bowl with the potato. Add the olive oil and the remaining lemon juice to the bowl. Toss and season with salt and pepper to taste. Top with the parsley leaves.

Serve at once from the bowl. Or divide among 4 salad plates.

WINE SUGGESTION: **Chardonnay, "Castello della Sala"–Antinori**

viareggina

This salad was created in Viareggio, a resort town in northern Tuscany. It's very simple, but the contrast of the crunchy hearts of palm and the smooth, creamy, avocado is all you need for a memorable dish. This is a great, quick salad to enjoy outdoors in the summer.

serves 4

2 fresh avocados

1 small head of Bibb lettuce or Boston lettuce, torn into bite-size pieces

1 head of radicchio, torn into bite-size pieces

1 can (14 oz/400g) hearts of palm packed in liquid, drained, and cut into 1-inch/2.5-cm pieces (see Note)

1 tablespoon olive oil

Fine sea salt

Freshly ground black pepper

Cut the avocados in half lengthwise and remove the pits using the heel of a chef's knife. Cut each avocado half into 2 or 3 long wedges, depending on the size of the avocado, then remove the skin.

Toss together the lettuce and radicchio in a small bowl. Spread them out to cover the surface of a platter or large plate.

Arrange the hearts of palm and avocado decoratively over the greens. Drizzle with the olive oil and season with salt and pepper to taste. Serve immediately.

NOTE: Use 8 ounces/225g fresh hearts of palm if you can find them.

WINE SUGGESTION: **Traminer Aromatico–Jermann**

rapini con salsiccia

BROCCOLI DI RAPA WITH SPICY PORK SAUSAGE

This is a classic, rustic Italian recipe in which bitter broccoli di rapa (see Note) and spicy sausage complement each other perfectly. The combination is also popular tossed with orecchiette, an ear-shaped pasta.

A lot of broccoli recipes tell you to blanch it, but you lose too much flavor that way. The way I cook broccoli, you cover it and let it steam and cook through right in the pan. The most important thing is to use the freshest broccoli di rapa available. Don't buy any that have yellow buds because they aren't old enough yet. Instead, choose broccoli that's bright green; it doesn't just look better; it tastes better, too.

SERVES 4

5 tablespoons olive oil

3 cloves garlic, smashed and peeled

2 pounds/900g broccoli di rapa, stems cut off and discarded

Fine sea salt

Freshly ground black pepper

¼ teaspoon crushed red pepper

4 small, spicy Italian pork sausages (4 oz/110g each), split lengthwise with halves attached by the skin

4 large sage leaves

Warm the olive oil over medium heat in a sauté pan wide and deep enough to hold the broccoli. Add the garlic. When the garlic has browned slightly, about 2 minutes, add the broccoli. Season with salt and pepper and sprinkle with the red pepper. If the broccoli looks dry, add a few tablespoons of water to the pan. Cover the pan immediately with a lid or inverted pan of the same size and cook for 3 to 7 minutes, depending on the size of the broccoli. Stop cooking as soon as the broccoli is cooked through; it shouldn't be mushy. If necessary, remove and taste a piece of broccoli to see if it's done. Transfer the broccoli to a bowl and cover it to keep it warm.

Add the split sausages to the pan, open side up. Place a sage leaf in the center of each open sausage. Cook for 2 minutes, then turn the sausages over, keeping the sage leaves in place. (They should adhere to the sausages.) I like to serve sausage with the skin on, but if the sausages begin to curl up as they cook, remove the skins using kitchen tongs. By this time, each pair of halves should have fused together into a rectangular block. Cook until warmed through, 3 to 4 minutes more.

Divide the broccoli among 4 salad plates and serve with 1 sausage (2 halves) on top of each mound of broccoli.

NOTE: Broccoli di rapa is small, bitter broccoli. You can eat the entire vegetable, leaves and all. A lot of people in English-speaking countries call this "broccoli rabe," but that's not the real word for it; I prefer to use the Italian term.

WINE SUGGESTION: **Terre di Tufi–Teruzzi & Puthod**

puNtareLLe

Puntarelle is a chicory that is in season from November through March. It looks like something out of a science fiction movie, but has a very fresh, clean taste and crunchy texture—like a cross between celery and Belgian endive. The anchovy-garlic sauce is my version of the traditional accompaniment.

SERVES 4

1 head of puntarelle (about 2 lb/900g)

6 tablespoons olive oil

1 clove garlic, peeled and minced

4 anchovy fillets

Splash red wine vinegar

Pull the outer green leaves off the puntarelle. Break the puntarelle into stalks and cut each stalk into ⅛-inch/0.25-cm-thick slivers. Set aside.

Pour the olive oil into a small sauté pan. Add the garlic and anchovy fillets and place over low heat. Cook, stirring with a wooden spoon, just until the anchovy falls apart, 3 to 4 minutes. Add a splash of red wine vinegar.

Pour the warm oil over the surface of a large plate or small platter and lay the puntarelle stalks on top. Serve at once.

PANZANeLLa

Italians are very resourceful people. Give us anything, even a loaf of stale bread, and we'll find something to do with it. In fact, stale bread is the basis for one of our favorite summer dishes—*panzanella*, a refreshing salad that's dressed with a lot of red wine vinegar to bring out the best flavor of the tomato, cucumbers, and peppers.

By the way, it turns out New Yorkers aren't that resourceful. It wasn't until Da Silvano opened that anyone served *panzanella* here. I can still remember the date: May 1, 1975.

serves 4

2 sweet red peppers

5 tablespoons olive oil

1 large loaf stale country bread, crusts removed and cut into 1-inch/2.5-cm cubes

3 tablespoons (loosely packed) fresh basil leaves

1 red onion, cut in half and then cut into ½-inch/1-cm slices

2 small cucumbers, peeled and cut into ½-inch/1-cm slices

2 vine-ripened tomatoes, cut into ½-inch/1-cm cubes

¼ cup/55ml red wine vinegar

Fine sea salt

Freshly ground black pepper

Rub each pepper with 1 tablespoon of the olive oil and roast over a gas flame until blackened on all sides, 3 to 4 minutes per side. Transfer the hot peppers to a paper bag and seal it. Let the peppers steam in their own heat to loosen the skins. When cool enough to handle, peel off the skin; it will come right off with the help of a paring knife. Cut the tops off the peppers and remove the seeds. Cut the peppers into 1-inch/2.5-cm-square pieces. Set aside.

Put the bread in a stainless steel bowl and drizzle a cup of cold water over it. Allow the bread to soak for 10 minutes. Squeeze the water out of the bread and return it to the dry bowl. Tear up the basil leaves and add them to the bowl with the bread. Add the pepper pieces, onion, cucumber, and tomato. Add the remaining olive oil and the vinegar. Season with salt and pepper. Toss well, taste, adjust the salt, pepper, and/or vinegar if necessary, and serve.

WINE SUGGESTION: **Pinot Grigio–Plozner**

BARBABIETOLE e INDIVIA

SALAD OF BEETS AND ENDIVE

This is not an Italian dish, but it does remind me of Florence because my grandmother used to serve us beets all the time. I made this recipe up in New York because I thought it would look pretty, which it does. But it also tastes delicious—the cool, crunchy, clean endive is the perfect foil for the sweet, tender beets.

SERVES 4

4 large red beets

Fine sea salt

4 medium Belgian endive

¼ cup/55ml Vinaigrette Modo Mio (page 186)

Freshly ground black pepper

Bring a large pot of water to a boil. Add the beets to the pot, and boil until they are done, about 1 hour 15 minutes. Salt the water about 15 minutes before the beets are done. To test for doneness, insert a sharp, thin-bladed knife into a beet; when it slips easily in and out, the beets are done. Use tongs or a slotted spoon to remove the beets from the water and set them aside to cool.

When cool enough to handle, transfer them to a cutting board. Peel the beets and slice them into ½-inch/1-cm rounds. Cut ½ inch/1 cm off the bottom of each Belgian endive and roughly chop the portion you've removed. Set aside. Separate the remaining endive into individual leaves.

Arrange the endive leaves in a circular pattern with the pointy ends facing outward on each of 4 salad plates. Lay the beet slices on top of the endive in a circular pattern maintaining a border of endive around the edges. Place some of the reserved, chopped endive in the center of the beets. Drizzle vinaigrette over the beets and the endive. Season with salt and pepper and serve.

WINE SUGGESTION: **"Fosarin"–Ronco dei Tassi**

OSTRICHE

Sometimes nothing is more refreshing than oysters, and there's an incredible variety to choose from here in the United States. I prefer those from the Pacific Northwest.

This is one of the few times I turn to French tradition because a *mignonette* is my favorite accompaniment to fresh oysters—the bite of shallots and pepper and the tang of vinegar is the perfect dressing. I have altered the classic recipe, which features ground black pepper, to suit my own affection for fresh green and yellow peppers. See if you don't agree that this way is better.

SERVES 4

1 teaspoon minced shallot

1 tablespoon minced green pepper

1 tablespoon minced yellow pepper

¼ cup/55ml red wine vinegar

Crushed ice

24 small Pacific oysters, preferably Kumomoto but Atlantic or Blue Point can be substituted, shucked, top shells removed, rinsed, dried, and reserved (see Sidebar)

Place a large circular platter in the refrigerator to chill.

Place the shallot and green and yellow peppers in a small ceramic or stainless steel mixing bowl. Add the vinegar and stir. Transfer the *mignonette* to a serving cup or bowl small enough to fit in the center of the platter.

Remove the platter from the refrigerator. Create a bed of crushed ice in the center of the platter. Arrange the oysters in a circular pattern on top of the crushed ice, leaving the center of the platter clear, and using the top shells for decoration if you like.

Drizzle a little *mignonette* over each oyster, then place the remaining *mignonette* in the center of the platter. Serve at once.

WINE SUGGESTION: **Prosecco–Canella**

HOW TO SHUCK OYSTERS

Grasp the oysters, one by one, cupped side down, firmly in one hand, using a towel to cover and protect the hand. With your free hand, insert a small, sharp knife into the oyster at the hinge. Wriggle the knife in the oyster, working it around until the shell opens, being careful not to let the knife slip out. Force open and remove the upper shell, reserving it for decoration if you like. Use the knife to loosen the oyster muscle from the shell. Either serve the oyster on the half-shell, or remove the oysters and store them in their liquid, discarding the shells. Fishmongers will usually shuck oysters for you, but it takes time, so call ahead.

GUESTS   St. Patrick's Day 1998

Silvano —
your corn beef and cabbage
is just so italian —
with love and
baci
Emma Thompson

ostriche fritte

This is another way to enjoy oysters, more for their texture than their flavor. The contrast of the fried *panata* coating and the soft, salty oysters is delicious, and the lemons keep them refreshing and light.

SERVES 4

24 oysters, preferably
Kumomoto but Atlantic or Blue
Point can be substituted,
shucked, shells rinsed, dried,
and reserved

1 cup/100g Panata (page 190)

2 teaspoons cornmeal

3 tablespoons olive oil

1 lemon, cut into wedges

Arrange the reserved oyster shells on a platter and set aside.

Place the *panata*, cornmeal, and 1 tablespoon of the olive oil in a small ceramic or stainless steel bowl and stir together. Roll the oysters in the mixture to coat them well.

Warm the remaining olive oil in a wide sauté pan over medium-high heat. When the oil is hot but not smoking, add the oysters to the pan. Fry for 1 to 2 minutes on each side. Using tongs or a slotted spoon, remove the oysters to paper towels to drain.

Place 1 fried oyster on each shell and serve hot with lemon wedges alongside.

WINE SUGGESTION: **Vermentino di Sardegna–Cantina Santadi**

seppie aLLa GRIGLIa

GRILLED CUTTLEFISH

Cuttlefish looks like a lot like squid, but it's much more satisfying. Dress the cuttlefish just before grilling; if you allow it to marinate, the acid in the lemon juice will begin to "cook" it.

SERVES 4

1 pound/450g cuttlefish, cleaned

2 tablespoons olive oil, plus more for oiling the grill grate

1 clove garlic, minced

Juice of ½ a lemon

1 lemon, cut into 4 wedges

Build a fire in an outdoor grill and let it burn until the coals are covered with white ash.

When the grill is ready, pour the olive oil into a small ceramic or stainless steel bowl. Add the garlic and lemon juice and stir. Place the cuttlefish in the bowl and toss briefly to coat, but do not allow it to soak.

Oil the grill grate. (See Note.)

Place the cuttlefish on the grill and cook for 3 to 4 minutes on each side.

Transfer to a platter, or divide among individual salad plates. Serve immediately, with lemon wedges alongside.

NOTE: Here's a trick a lot of chefs use when oiling their grills: Keep a small bowl of oil by your side at the grill. Take a small, clean towel, bunch it up and tie it in a bundle with kitchen string. Keep that in the bowl and when you need to refresh the oil on the grate, use long tongs to pick up the towel and run it over the grate. This is a good way to stay far away from the flame when oiling your grill.

WINE SUGGESTION: **Afix Riesling–Jermann**

carpaccio Di coda Di rospo e melone cantaloupe

MONKFISH AND MELON CARPACCIO

I thought of this recipe when visiting St. Tropez. At dinner one night, they served us a carpaccio of monkfish to start, and after dinner they served a carpaccio of melon for dessert. When I thought back on the meal, I remembered both flavors so fondly that I decided to combine them in one dish.

This recipe works because monkfish is so meaty. When you think about it, this carpaccio isn't that different from an Italian classic: prosciutto and melon.

1 pound/450g boneless, sushi-grade monkfish fillet

1 ripe cantaloupe (about 2 lb/900g) or French *cavaillon* melon where available

½ lemon

2 tablespoons olive oil

SERVES 4

Place 4 dinner plates in the refrigerator to chill.

Wrap the monkfish in plastic wrap and place it in the freezer for 20 to 30 minutes to chill it and firm it up.

Slice the monkfish crosswise into paper-thin slices using a slicing machine and arrange the slices between sheets of wax paper. Place them in the refrigerator to keep them cold while you slice the melon (see Note).

Cut the melon in half, remove the seeds, cut off the skin, and cut the melon into ¼-inch/0.5-cm-thick slices, each about 1-inch/2.5-cm square.

On each of 4 plates, decoratively arrange the monkfish slices next to one another to cover the plate. Place a melon-square on top of each monkfish slice. Squeeze some lemon juice and drizzle some olive oil over each carpaccio. Serve immediately.

NOTE: If you don't have a slicing machine, use a very sharp knife and keep your hand as steady as possible to cut the fish. Place each hand-cut monkfish slice between sheets of plastic wrap and pound with a meat tenderizer or the bottom of a heavy pan until paper-thin. Reserve the slices in the refrigerator.

WINE SUGGESTION: **Müller-Thurgau**

sarde alla griglia

GRILLED SARDINES

A lot of my customers are surprised by how much they like fresh sardines, which have nothing in common with the oily canned fish many Americans picture when they think of them. I learned to appreciate sardines when I was a chef in Bimini years ago. Cooked outside over the flame of an open grill, they brought together everything I loved about the island—the open air, the fresh seafood, and the simplicity. Come to think of it, Bimini reminded me of the Italian Riviera.

Be careful not to let the grill get too hot when you're cooking these. (If you have a grill with an adjustable coal bed or grate, keep a good distance between the coals and the fish.) If the sardines do begin to stick, gently loosen them with a spatula.

If you want a smoky flavor in the finished dish, cook the sardines with the grill cover closed. You can also prepare these indoors on a grill pan or cast-iron skillet on the stovetop.

serves 4

8 fresh Portuguese sardines, gutted with heads intact, prepared by your fishmonger

5 tablespoons olive oil, plus more for oiling the grill grate

2 cups/225g Panata (page 190)

1 lemon, halved

1 lemon, cut into thin slices

3 tablespoons minced flat-leaf parsley

Prepare an outdoor grill, letting the coals burn until covered with white ash.

Use your fingers to spread ½ tablespoon of olive oil over the skin of each sardine. Roll the sardines in the *panata*, pressing down a bit to make sure the coating sticks.

Carefully oil the grill grate.

Place the fish on the grill with a few inches/centimetres between them. (Work in batches if you have to, reapplying oil to the grate between batches.) Grill 2 to 4 minutes per side, keeping a close eye on the sardines because if they start to burn, they will turn to a crisp before you know it.

Remove the sardines from the grill, place them on a platter, drizzle them with the remaining olive oil, squeeze the halved lemon over them, and scatter the minced parsley over the platter. Serve with the slices of lemon alongside.

WINE SUGGESTION: **Sauvignon–Bortoluzzi**

poLenta coL goRgonzoLa

POLENTA WITH GORGONZOLA

Rich, creamy gorgonzola and the coarse cornmeal of polenta are a match made in heaven. Because they are so very different in taste and texture, each calls your attention to the qualities of the other.

Fine sea salt

1 tablespoon olive oil

8 ounces/225g (1 ¼ cups) quick-cooking polenta

2 ounces/55g Gorgonzola

serves 6 to 8

Bring 1 quart/1 litre of salted water and the olive oil to a boil in a pot large enough to hold the polenta. Slowly add the polenta, stirring or whisking it in as you do. Lower the heat and cook the polenta over low heat for 5 to 6 minutes, stirring frequently to prevent scorching.

About 1 minute before the polenta is done, remove the cheese from the refrigerator and cut it into small cubes.

Scatter the cheese cubes over the polenta and stir it in as it melts. Divide the polenta among individual plates and serve immediately.

fogLie DI saLvia fritte

When I was a little boy, my mother made these fried sage leaves, and when I think of those days, their flavor still haunts my palate. These are perfect with cocktails or a beer, and they can also be used to garnish dishes, especially those featuring rabbit. Use white pepper if you have it so that it doesn't show, and be careful not to overheat the oil or you'll scorch the leaves.

In Italy, this recipe is made with gigantic sage leaves. It's difficult to find such large ones here, but use the largest ones you can find; they'll still taste delicious.

serves 4

1 egg, separated

1 cup/140g all-purpose flour

½ cup/110ml milk

½ cup/110ml beer

Sea salt

Freshly ground pepper, preferably white

2 cups/450ml vegetable oil

24 large sage leaves

Whip the egg white in a stainless steel bowl, until it forms stiff peaks.

In another large bowl, whisk together the flour, milk, and egg yolk. Whisk the beer into the flour-milk-egg mixture, then gently fold in the egg white until thoroughly incorporated. Season the batter with salt and pepper.

Warm the oil in a deep-sided pan wide enough to hold the sage leaves in a single layer over medium heat. (If you don't have a wide enough pan, make these in 2 or 3 batches.)

Dip each leaf in the batter to coat it thoroughly. When the oil is hot but not smoking, lower the leaves into the oil, one at a time, working quickly to ensure even cooking and being careful not to crowd the leaves. Fry 60 to 90 seconds, or until lightly golden brown, then use tongs to flip the leaves and cook the other side for about 1 minute. Remove the leaves with a slotted spoon and place on paper towels to absorb the excess oil.

Serve hot or at room temperature.

funghi trifolati

SAUTÉED PORCINI MUSHROOMS WITH MINT

I love sautéed porcini mushrooms that have been tossed with *nepetella*, an Italian herb that's unavailable in the United States. Here, they are tossed with the next best thing, mint, which lightens up their deep, woodsy flavor.

Properly cooked porcini mushrooms should be meaty, and firm enough that you need a knife to cut them. You can serve them on their own to begin a meal, spoon them over toasted bread that's been rubbed with garlic (making a *crostini funghi*), or on top of polenta.

½ cup/110ml olive oil, plus more if needed

2 garlic cloves, peeled and left whole

1 pound/450g fresh porcini mushrooms, wiped clean with a damp cloth or paper towel, base of stem trimmed, and cut into ¼-inch/0.5-cm slices

Fine sea salt

Freshly ground black pepper

3 tablespoons (loosely packed) whole mint leaves

serves 4

Warm the olive oil in a deep-sided sauté pan large enough to hold the mushrooms over medium heat. Add the garlic and cook for 1 minute to infuse the oil with flavor. Add the mushrooms and season with salt and pepper. Cook, tossing the mushrooms constantly, for 4 to 5 minutes. If the mushrooms begin to dry out, add another tablespoon or so of olive oil. Remove the pan from the heat, add the mint leaves, and toss. Pick out and discard the garlic. Taste and adjust the seasoning if necessary.

Divide the mushrooms among 4 small plates, or serve family-style from a large bowl.

WINE SUGGESTION: **Barbera Superiore–Bricco Mondalino**

VULCANO SILVANO

SILVANO'S VOLCANO

This dish is called Vulcano Silvano because the mound of mashed potatoes with melted cheese and shaved mushrooms on top looks like a volcano that's running over with lava.

It's funny how restaurant recipes come into being. This one was born when one of my waiters, Filippo, saw me eating some mashed potatoes after lunch one day. "Hey, Silvano," he said, "how about shaving some cheese over the potatoes?" I thought it was a good idea and then I said, "Add some porcini and pepper."

SERVES 4

Fine sea salt

2 pounds/900g Yukon Gold potatoes

1 cup/225ml whole milk

4 tablespoons/110g (½ stick) unsalted butter

Fine sea salt

Freshly ground black pepper

16 fresh basil leaves

1 cup/110g thinly shaved Parmigiano-Reggiano

1 tablespoon olive oil

4 large fresh porcini mushrooms, thinly sliced

Fill a pot large enough to hold the potatoes with water. Salt the water and bring to a boil over high heat. Place the potatoes in the boiling water and cook for 20 to 30 minutes, or until tender. (Test for doneness by inserting a sharp, thin-bladed knife into 1 potato.) Drain the potatoes and allow to cool.

When the potatoes are cool enough to handle, remove the skins using a paring knife. Pass the potatoes through a ricer or mash them with a masher, being careful not to overwork them. Set the potatoes aside in a large, stainless steel bowl.

Pour the milk into a small pot and bring to a boil over high heat. As soon as it boils, carefully pour the milk over the potatoes. Add the butter, season with salt and pepper, and carefully stir with a wooden spoon until a purée is formed. Taste and adjust the seasoning if necessary.

Divide the purée among 4 small plates, forming a mound in the center of each plate. Stick 4 basil leaves into each mound of potato purée so that they stand up, and scatter the mushrooms over the potatoes. Sprinkle each mound of potato purée with a ¼ cup of cheese, then drizzle each with a little olive oil and grind some black pepper over them. Work as quickly as possible so the food is hot when it gets to the table.

WINE SUGGESTION: **Gavi di Gavi–La Scolca**

fagottini tartufati

LITTLE TRUFFLED BUNDLES

This is a variation on carpaccio in which you put the cheese and *rucola* inside the beef and roll it up into a little bundle. I make this extra special by adding truffle oil and fresh truffles, but if you don't have any truffles (or don't want to spend the money for them), you can leave them out and the *fagottini* will still be delicious.

SERVES 4

8 paper-thin slices eye round beef

2 tablespoons white truffle oil

4 tablespoons freshly grated Parmigiano-Reggiano

8 tablespoons (loosely packed) rucola, roughly chopped

¼ ounce/7 to 8g fresh white truffle from Alba

Spread 1 slice of beef out on a clean, dry work surface. Drizzle a few drops of truffle oil over the beef and use your fingers or the back of a spoon to evenly distribute it. Spoon ½ tablespoon Parmigiano and 1 tablespoon *rucola* in the center of the beef. Gather up the ends of the beef and fold into a little bundle, sealing the Parmigiano and *rucola* inside. Turn the bundle over so that it cannot open. Repeat the steps with the remaining beef, cheese, and *rucola*.

To serve, place 2 *fagottini* on each of 4 salad plates. Drizzle some truffle oil over each one and shave some fresh truffle over the top.

WINE SUGGESTION: **Barbera–Monti**

panzanella di farro

FARRO SALAD

This is a variation on the classic Panzanella (page 23), which substitutes farro (known as spelt in this country) for bread. Farro is a very durable grain that should be cooked just until al dente so it retains its flavor and texture. Because farro will not become soggy, I've made this recipe larger than most of the others in the book. It's ideal for a picnic or other large gathering and can be kept, covered, in the refrigerator for a day or two if you have leftovers.

You need to soak the farro for two hours before cooking it, so be sure to plan ahead.

SERVES 8

8 ounces/225g (1 cup) farro

1 celery stalk, cut into 3 to 4 large pieces

1 large carrot, peeled and cut into 3 to 4 large pieces

1 red onion, quartered

1 cup/225g fresh basil leaves, loosely packed

1 red onion, cut in half and then into thin slices

2 small cucumbers, peeled and sliced into ½-inch/1-cm rounds

2 vine-ripened tomatoes, quartered

Soak the farro in cold water for 2 hours. Drain well in several changes of cold water to remove any grit.

Bring a large pot of salted water to a boil. Add the celery, carrot, and quartered onion to the pot. Add the farro and simmer until al dente, 35 to 45 minutes. Drain the farro, refresh under cold running water for 15 seconds, and transfer to a large bowl to cool. As soon as it is cool enough to touch, pick out and discard the celery, carrot, and onion.

Tear the basil into bite-size pieces.

Add the basil, sliced onion, cucumbers, and tomatoes to the cool farro. Add the olive oil and vinegar and toss. Season with salt and pepper and

3 tablespoons olive oil

¼ cup/55ml red wine vinegar,
plus more if necessary

Fine sea salt

Freshly ground black pepper

toss again. Taste and add more vinegar if it doesn't yet have a nice, strong, tangy flavor.

Cover and refrigerate for at least 1 hour. Serve cold.

WINE SUGGESTION: **Tocai Friulano–Villa Russiz**

pasta, risotti, e zuppe

PASTA, RISOTTO, AND SOUP

What are these three types of recipes doing together in one chapter? I've grouped them because it's unlikely that you'll have more than one of them in the same meal. You might have an appetizer, then one of these dishes, then a meat dish of some kind. Or perhaps you'll have one of these dishes as the appetizer, and then move on to the main course.

The pastas feature a lot of very traditional ones, including *Spaghetti Puttanesca*, *Linguine alle Vongole*, *Tortellini alla Panna*, *Penne Arrabbiata*, *Ravioli bella Firenze*, and *Bucatini con le Sarde*. If they're so traditional, why are they in my book? Because every Italian has his or her own way of cooking a dish, and these are my ways. For example, I don't rinse my capers or anchovies before using them; I don't put a ton of red pepper in my *arrabbiata* sauce (or in any sauce), and I add chopped tomatoes to my linguine with clams, even though I favor a white sauce. Those things all make a difference. They make these recipes my own, even though the names are very common.

But there *are* a few pastas of my own invention here, including *Rigatoni Focaccia* and *Taglierini con Ricci di Mare e Avocado*, featuring sea urchin and avocado (I got the idea eating sushi one night).

My biggest advice when it comes to pasta is to keep it al dente (when using dried pasta). Taste it as it's cooking and as soon as it seems cooked, drain it and toss it with the sauce. In time, you'll find that you enjoy it cooked less and less, the way I do.

There are just a few risotti, all of them fairly classic—Risotto ai Carciofi, Risotto alle Vongole, and Risotto alla Milanese. People don't think of risotto as al dente, but that's how you want it to come out as well. The overall dish should be creamy, but the individual grains of rice should still have some bite to them.

Our soups are very complex and satisfying, and not just in the cold months, when we serve the mushroom soup, Zuppa di Funghi; the sausage soup, Zuppa alla Porcara; the Tuscan classics Ribollita and Zuppa di Farro, as well as other time-honored soups. We also sell many popular summer soups including the tomato and bread soup called Pappa al Pomodoro, my version of the Spanish classic, Gazpacho Modo Mio, and Pasta e Fagioli, or pasta and bean soup, which is as good hot in the winter as it is cool in the summer.

pasta aL Limone

LEMON PASTA

I'm not the first person who ever made this dish, but I'm the only one I know who squeezes lemon juice into the pasta water. I began doing this when I accidentally dropped a lemon in a pot of cooking linguine and found that it gave the pasta itself the taste of lemon. This is a perfect, refreshing dish for a summer night. If you like, save some lemon zest (or, better yet, grate some extra) and sprinkle it on top of each serving.

2 lemons

Fine sea salt

1 pound/450g dried linguine

2 tablespoons unsalted butter

½ cup/110ml heavy cream

2 tablespoons freshly grated
Parmigiano-Reggiano

Freshly ground black pepper

SERVES 4 TO 6

Using the finest holes of a grater, remove the zest from the lemons, taking care to avoid the white pith, which is very bitter. Reserve the zest.

Using a sharp, thin-bladed knife, carefully remove and discard the pith from the lemons. Cut the lemons in half and remove as many seeds as you can without squeezing the lemons and losing juice.

Fill a large pot with salted water. Squeeze the lemons into the pot, then drop the lemons into the water. Bring the water to a boil over high heat. Add the linguine and cook until al dente, about 7 minutes.

After the linguine has been cooking for about 5 minutes, melt the butter in a sauté pan wide and deep enough to hold the pasta over medium-high heat. Add the cream and stir. Add the lemon zest and stir again. Season with a pinch of salt.

When the linguine is done, drain it and add it to the pan with the lemon-cream sauce. Sprinkle the Parmigiano over the pasta and cook, tossing the pasta with the sauce, for 1 minute. Serve in individual bowls, topping each serving with black pepper.

WINE SUGGESTION: **Vernaccia–Teruzzi & Puthod**

penne arrabbiata

SPICY PENNE

The name of this dish in Italian literally means angry or mad. I don't feel that way when I leave my restaurant every night, but this is one of my favorite late-night dinners when I come home exhausted from work. It can be thrown together very quickly and makes a big impact with lots of spicy flavor.

SERVES 4 to 6

Fine sea salt

5 tablespoons olive oil

2 cloves garlic, crushed and peeled

1 can (28 oz/800g) whole plum tomatoes, preferably San Marzano, crushed by hand

½ teaspoon crushed red pepper, or more to taste

1 pound/450g dried penne or ziti or rigatoni

Bring a large pot of salted water to a boil over high heat.

Pour the olive oil into a deep-sided sauté pan large enough to hold the tomatoes and penne and warm the oil over medium heat. Add the garlic and cook until lightly browned, about 2 minutes. Remove the pan from the stove and slowly add the tomatoes, being careful not to let them splatter when they meet the hot oil. Add the crushed red pepper and return the pan to the heat. Cook for about 15 minutes.

When the water reaches a rolling boil, add the penne, cover the pot to return to a boil, then cook, uncovered, until al dente, about 10 minutes.

While the sauce is cooking, taste it and add salt and more red pepper if you like.

Drain the pasta and carefully add it to the sauce. Cook the penne in the sauce, tossing, for 1 minute.

Serve the pasta family-style from a serving bowl, or divide it among individual bowls and spoon any extra sauce over the top of each serving.

WINE SUGGESTION: **Brunello di Montalcino–Lisini**

spaghetti puttanesca

This is another pasta dish that's very easy to prepare. The thing I love about it is that if you have a well-stocked pantry—pasta, capers, anchovies, olives, canned tomatoes—then you can make this whenever you desire it. (In fact, the name of this dish actually means "whore's pasta," so called because they say prostitutes prepared it for themselves between visits from "clients.") Before I opened Da Silvano, my friends used to ask me to cook at parties a lot, and this was usually the dish I made. It takes very little time and effort, just enough for your appetite to build.

SERVES 4 to 6

⅓ cup/75ml olive oil

3 cloves garlic, smashed and peeled

2 cloves garlic, minced

4 anchovy fillets

1 tablespoon capers, drained but not rinsed

2 tablespoons roughly chopped pitted Greek olives (see Note)

1 can (28 oz/800g) high-quality Italian plum tomatoes, drained and roughly chopped

Fine sea salt

1 pound/450g spaghetti

4 tablespoons minced flat-leaf parsley

Freshly ground black pepper

Warm the olive oil in a sauté pan wide and deep enough to hold all the ingredients, including the pasta, over medium heat. Add the 3 smashed garlic cloves and cook until golden brown, 2 to 3 minutes. Remove the garlic from the pan and discard it. Add the minced garlic, anchovies, capers, olives, and tomatoes. Toss together, lower the heat, and cook for 5 to 10 minutes.

While the sauce is cooking, bring a large pot of salted water to a boil over high heat. Add the spaghetti, cover the pot to return to the boil, then cook, uncovered, until the spaghetti is al dente, about 8 minutes.

Drain the spaghetti and add it to the pan with the sauce. Toss. Add the parsley and season with black pepper. Toss again and sauté for about 30 seconds.

Serve from a large serving bowl, or divide among individual bowls.

NOTE: It may surprise you to learn that I use Greek rather than Italian olives, but I think Greek olives have more flavor because they are soaked in sea water and then dried in the sun.

WINE SUGGESTION: **Cuvee, "Christian Bernard"–Costaripa**

BUCATINI CON Le saRDe

BUCATINI WITH SARDINES

When my father was an officer in the Italian army, we lived for a time in the barracks. The officer next door was Sicilian, and his wife made this dish all the time with her windows open. I fell in love with it long before I ever tasted it—from the aroma wafting through the army base.

Bucatini is a long, tubular pasta. It is similar to perciatelli.

serves 4 to 6

Fine sea salt

4 tablespoons olive oil

1 small red onion, roughly chopped

1 pound/450g dried bucatini

1 cup/115g dried breadcrumbs

4 medium plum tomatoes, roughly chopped

8 fresh Portuguese sardines (about 4 oz/110g each), cleaned, gutted, filleted, and cut into 1-inch/2.5-cm pieces

¼ teaspoon crushed red pepper

1 fennel bulb (about 12 oz/340g), hollow stems removed, roughly chopped

2 tablespoons golden raisins

¾ cup/170g Sugo di Pomodoro (page 182)

Preheat the oven to 350°F/180°C/gas 4.

Bring a large pot of salted water to a boil over high heat.

Warm the olive oil in a sauté pan wide and deep enough to hold all the ingredients, including the pasta, over medium heat. Add the onion and cook until lightly colored, about 7 minutes.

When the water is boiling, add the bucatini and cook until al dente, about 10 minutes.

Meanwhile, spread the breadcrumbs out on a nonstick cookie sheet, spread the chopped tomatoes over them, and bake until the crumbs are warmed and the tomato has soaked into them, about 10 minutes.

While the pasta and breadcrumbs are cooking, add the sardines, red pepper, chopped fennel, and raisins to the pan with the onions. Stir gently and cook for 2 minutes. Add the sugo to the pan, stir, and cook for 2 minutes more.

Drain the bucatini and add it to the sauce. Toss and cook for 30 seconds.

Remove the cookie sheet with the tomato and breadcrumbs from the oven.

Divide the bucatini among large serving bowls and spoon some of the tomato-breadcrumb mixture over each serving.

WINE SUGGESTION: **Chardonnay–Antinori**

Linguine alle vongole

LINGUINE WITH CLAMS

There are two ways to make linguine with clams—in a white sauce (just olive oil and wine, really) and in a red tomato sauce. Most Italians prefer the white sauce because it lets the flavor and texture of the clams shine through. I'm the same way, but I do add some tomato (rather than sauce) for a little extra flavor and acidity.

SERVES 4 TO 6

Fine sea salt

6 tablespoons olive oil

2 cloves garlic, crushed and peeled

60 small clams, preferably from New Zealand

¼ teaspoon crushed red pepper, or more to taste

1 teaspoon dried oregano leaves

2 plum tomatoes, quartered

1 pound/450g dried linguine

½ cup/110ml dry white wine

6 tablespoons minced flat-leaf parsley

Bring a large pot of salted water to a boil.

Warm 4 tablespoons of the olive oil in a pan wide and deep enough to hold the pasta and the clams over medium heat. Add the garlic and cook until it browns, about 5 minutes. Add the clams, red pepper, and oregano to the pan. Add the tomatoes and cover the pan with a lid or an inverted pan of the same size.

When the water is boiling, add the linguine and cook until al dente, about 7 minutes.

Cook the sauce, covered, until the clams open, 4 to 5 minutes. Pour the wine over the open clams, then turn off the heat. Use tongs to discard any clams that have not opened.

As soon as the linguine is al dente, drain it and add it to the pan with the clams. Place the pan over medium heat and sauté for 1 minute. Taste and add more red pepper, if desired. Drizzle with the remaining olive oil and scatter the minced parsley over the top.

Turn the contents of the pan out into a large serving bowl, spooning all the sauce from the pan over the top, or divide among individual bowls and spoon some sauce from the bottom of the pan over each serving. For the best presentation, use tongs to transfer the pasta to the bowl or bowls first, then pour the clams over the top or place them over the top of each serving using the tongs. Provide an empty bowl for your guests to dispose of their shells.

WINE SUGGESTION: **Pinot Grigio–Villa Russiz**

tortellini alla panna

TORTELLINI WITH CREAM SAUCE

The best tortellini I ever had was in a very unlikely place, a buffet-style restaurant at the train station in Florence where they served meat tortellini tossed with hot cream. At Da Silvano, we use tortellini filled with a combination of prosciutto and mortadella, but you can use any meat tortellini.

SERVES 4 TO 6

Fine sea salt

1 pound/450g meat tortellini, at room temperature

1 tablespoon unsalted butter

1 cup/225ml heavy cream

¼ cup/30g freshly grated Parmigiano-Reggiano

Freshly ground black pepper

Bring a large pot of salted water to a boil. Add the tortellini and cook until al dente, about 6 minutes.

A few minutes before the pasta is done, melt the butter in a pan wide and deep enough to hold the tortellini and cream over medium heat. Add the cream and bring it to a simmer.

Drain the tortellini and add it to the butter and cream. Cook, stirring, to keep the cream from scorching against the bottom of the pan, for 1 minute. Stir in the Parmigiano and season with pepper.

Serve family-style from a large serving bowl, or divide among individual bowls.

WINE SUGGESTION: **Pinot Grigio–Villa Russiz**

ravioli bella firenze

RAVIOLI IN THE STYLE OF BEAUTIFUL FLORENCE

The powerful flavor of sage, tossed with hot butter, is the perfect complement to ricotta and cheese ravioli. You really need only enough butter to coat the ravioli and distribute the flavor of the herb, but if you prefer a richer dish, add another tablespoon.

Fine sea salt

1 pound/450g spinach and ricotta ravioli, fresh or frozen (available from pasta shops and specialty grocers)

1 tablespoon unsalted butter

4 to 6 fresh sage leaves

Freshly ground black pepper

¼ cup/30g freshly grated Parmigiano-Reggiano

serves 4 to 6

Bring a large pot of salted water to a boil. Add the ravioli and cook until done, 1 to 2 minutes for fresh or 3 to 4 minutes for frozen. When the ravioli rise to the top of the pot, they are done. (See Note.)

About 1 minute before the ravioli are done, melt the butter in a sauté pan large enough to hold the ravioli over medium heat. Let the butter turn golden brown, but do not burn it. When the ravioli are done, use a slotted spoon to transfer them to the pan with the butter. Add the sage leaves and toss the ingredients together as they cook for 1 minute. Season the ravioli with salt and pepper.

Serve the ravioli family-style from a large serving bowl, or divide among individual bowls. Sprinkle Parmigiano over the top or serve alongside at the table.

NOTE: There's no need to defrost frozen ravioli; just add them frozen to the hot water. It will take less time to cook them than to wait for them to come to room temperature, and they'll taste just as good.

WINE SUGGESTION: **Chardonnay "Libaio"–Ruffino**

tagliatelle al tartufo Bianco

TAGLIATELLE WITH WHITE TRUFFLES

Warren Beatty ordered this dish one night. When I asked him how he liked it, he said that it was delicious but that he wanted some more truffles. I explained that white truffles are very expensive and that I had already shaved half of one over his dish. "Give me eight orders worth of truffles," he said. It turned into a $500 plate of pasta.

serves 4 to 6

Fine sea salt

1 pound/450g fresh tagliatelle

2 tablespoons store-bought truffle butter, softened at room temperature

Splash of white truffle oil

¼ ounce/7 to 8g fresh white truffle from Alba

Bring a large pot of salted water to a boil. Add the tagliatelle and cook until done, about 3 minutes. Drain the pasta and return it to the hot pot. Add the truffle butter and a splash of truffle oil and toss well.

Divide among individual bowls and shave 6 to 8 truffle slices over each serving...unless you're Warren Beatty.

WINE SUGGESTION: **Chardonnay "Rossj-Bass"**–*Gaja*

taglierini empolese

Empoli is the artichoke capital of Tuscany with the very best artichokes I've ever had. You won't be able to get your hands on them here, but this dish will still be delicious.

serves 4 to 6

1 lemon, halved

6 baby artichokes

5 tablespoons olive oil

1 medium leek, white part only, well washed and cut into 1-inch/2.5-cm pieces

¼ teaspoon freshly ground black pepper, plus more to taste

Fine sea salt

1 pound/450g fresh taglierini

½ cup/55g freshly grated Parmigiano-Reggiano

Fill a stainless steel or ceramic bowl large enough to hold the artichokes with cold water. Squeeze the juice from the lemon halves into the bowl.

Clean and trim the artichokes by cutting off the stems and snapping back and removing all the tough outer leaves. As they are prepared, place the artichokes in the bowl with the lemon water to keep them from discoloring.

Remove the artichokes from the water, one by one. Cut each one in half lengthwise, then slice each half lengthwise as thin as possible, patting the slices dry with paper towels and collecting them in a dry bowl.

Warm the olive oil in a pan wide and deep enough to hold all the ingredients over medium heat. Add the artichoke slices, leek, and black pepper, toss, and sauté for 5 minutes. Turn off the heat and leave the ingredients in the pan.

Bring a large pot of salted water to a boil. Add the taglierini and cook until done, about 3 minutes.

Drain the taglierini and add it to the pan with the artichokes, toss well, and cook over medium heat for 30 seconds. Add the Parmigiano and toss again.

Serve the pasta family-style from a large serving bowl, or divide among individual bowls.

WINE SUGGESTION: **Vernaccia di San Gimignano–Teruzzi & Puthod**

Gnocchi all' aragosta

GNOCCHI WITH LOBSTER

This recipe illustrates how simple cooking can be when you bring together a few ingredients that were meant for each other. Be careful not to overcook the lobster; it can toughen up very easily.

SERVES 4 to 6

2 live lobsters (1½ lb/675g each)

Fine sea salt

70 to 80 gnocchi (recipe follows)

5 tablespoons olive oil

1 shallot, peeled and thinly sliced

2 plum tomatoes, cut into ¼-inch/0.5-cm dice

¼ teaspoon crushed red pepper

Splash of dry white wine

3 tablespoons minced flat-leaf parsley

Bring a pot of water large enough to hold the lobsters to a boil over high heat. Add the lobsters, cover the pot, and cook for 8 to 10 minutes. Remove the lobsters from the pot and set aside to cool.

While the lobsters are cooling, bring a large pot of salted water to a boil over high heat.

When the lobsters are cool enough to handle, remove the meat from the body and claws. Cut the meat into bite-size pieces.

Add the gnocchi to the boiling salted water and cook until they rise to the surface, about 5 minutes.

Meanwhile, warm the olive oil in a sauté pan deep and wide enough to hold all of the ingredients over medium heat. Add the shallot and cook until golden brown, about 3 minutes. Add the tomatoes and cook for 2 minutes. Add the lobster, red pepper, and wine. Cook for 2 minutes, but no longer or the lobster meat will toughen.

Turn off the heat under both the gnocchi and the lobster sauce. Transfer the gnocchi to the sauté pan using a slotted spoon. Add the parsley, season with salt, and toss.

Serve family-style from a large serving bowl, or divide among individual bowls.

WINE SUGGESTION: **Müller-Thurgau**

GNOCCHI

When you buy gnocchi in stores, it's often so heavy that it makes you uncomfortably full. But properly made gnocchi are light and fluffy. The key is not to overwork the potatoes—mash them just enough, knead the dough just enough, and roll the individual pieces just enough. As soon as each step is completed, stop.

Gnocchi can be enjoyed with simple toppings like butter and cheese, chopped fresh tomatoes, or shaved truffles, as well as lobster sauce.

1½ pounds/675g Yukon Gold potatoes

Fine sea salt

8 ounces/225g (about 1 ¾ cups) all-purpose flour

1 egg, at room temperature

makes 1¼ pound/565g dough, 70 to 80 gnocchi

Place the potatoes in a pot and cover them by 1 to 2 inches/2.5 to 5 cm with cold water. Salt the water and place the pot over high heat. Bring the water to a boil and cook until the potatoes are done, 15 to 20 minutes. Test the potatoes for doneness by inserting a sharp, thin-bladed knife into them.

Drain the potatoes and allow them to cool.

Peel the potatoes using a paring knife and transfer them to a large bowl. Crush them with a masher, being careful not to overwork them.

Lightly flour a work surface and mound the potatoes in the center of it. Sprinkle the flour over the potatoes and gently knead them together. Make a well in the center of the potato-flour mound. Crack the egg into a small bowl, beat it, and pour it into the well. Use a fork to work the egg into the potato-flour mound. As soon as it is incorporated, begin using your hands to knead the dough until it is no longer sticky. Divide the dough into 6 equal portions.

Roll out each portion of dough, one by one, into a rope-like length ½ inch/1 cm in diameter. Re-flour the work surface periodically to keep the dough from sticking.

Cut each rope into 1-inch/2.5-cm pieces and roll each piece into a small ball. If you would like to create a ridged surface to catch sauces, roll each gnocchi off the back of a fork, pressing gently so the tines make an impression.

Cook the gnocchi in boiling salted water until they rise to the surface, about 5 minutes.

STORING EXTRA GNOCCHI

If not cooking the gnocchi immediately, it must be frozen. Place the gnocchi on a cookie sheet and transfer to the freezer. Let them harden over the course of 3 or 4 hours, then store them in a plastic bag in the freezer until ready to use.

rigatoni focaccia

RIGATONI WITH SMOKED BACON

Sometimes we describe this dish, inspired by the fillings of a sandwich popular in Florence, to customers at Da Silvano and they shriek. Bacon, cream, butter, and cheese—how could it possibly be good for you? It's not as heavy as it sounds, and the herb mixture makes it taste even lighter. Be sure to use rigatoni, which catches a lot of sauce.

serves 4 to 6

Fine sea salt

1 pound/450g rigatoni

2 sage leaves

3 sprigs of rosemary

1 clove garlic, smashed and peeled

8 ounces/225g double-smoked bacon, cut into ¼-inch/ 0.5-cm dice (see Mail-Order Sources)

Splash of dry white wine

4 plum tomatoes, coarsely chopped

1 cup/225ml heavy cream

1 tablespoon unsalted butter

¼ cup/30g freshly grated Parmigiano-Reggiano

2 tablespoons minced flat-leaf parsley

Freshly ground black pepper

Bring a large pot of salted water to a boil.

Add the rigatoni to the pot and cook until al dente, about 10 minutes.

While the rigatoni is cooking, chop the sage, rosemary, and garlic together into a thick paste. Set aside.

Warm a sauté pan wide and deep enough to hold all the ingredients over medium heat. Add the bacon and cook until some fat has rendered and it has just begun to brown and crisp, about 6 minutes. Add the sage-rosemary-garlic mixture, stir, and cook for 2 minutes. Add a splash of white wine to the pan and cook until the wine evaporates, 15 to 30 seconds. Add the tomatoes, stir, and cook for 2 to 3 minutes. Add the cream and butter and stir to incorporate.

Drain the rigatoni and add it to the pan with the sauce. Add the cheese, parsley, season with black pepper, and toss.

Serve family-style from a large serving bowl, or divide among individual bowls.

WINE SUGGESTION: **"Bricco del Drago"–Poderi Colla**

taglierini con ricci di mare e avocado

TAGLIERINI WITH SEA URCHINS AND AVOCADO

This recipe was inspired by a sushi dinner I enjoyed one night in New York City. I came to Da Silvano right after the meal and began playing around with some ingredients. This is the result.

SERVES 4 TO 6

Fine sea salt

1 pound/450g fresh taglierini

1 very ripe avocado, halved, pit removed with the heel of a chef's knife, peeled, and cut into thin wedges

16 to 24 shelled sea urchins (four per serving)

Olive oil

Freshly ground black pepper

Bring a large pot of salted water to a boil over high heat. Add the taglierini and cook until done, 2 to 3 minutes. Drain the taglierini and divide it among 4 to 6 plates.

Arrange the avocado wedges around the center of the pasta mounds. Place the sea urchins, four per plate, in the circle formed by the avocado tips.

Drizzle each dish with olive oil and black pepper and serve immediately.

WINE SUGGESTION: **Chardonnay, "Cabreo La Pietra"–Ruffino**

tagLiateLLe contadina

Peasant food is the heart of Tuscan cooking. For centuries the Tuscan people have learned to improvise with whatever they have on hand, and the results have become the stuff of legend. This recipe uses a little of everything, so I think it must've been created from leftovers—a few sausages, a cup of cream, some herbs, peas, and tomatoes. None of those ingredients is enough to be a meal on its own, but toss them with some pasta and they become a beautiful thing. If the people who invented this recipe saw people lining up for it in a restaurant hundreds of years later, they'd never stop laughing.

SERVES 4 to 6

Fine sea salt

4 sage leaves

1 sprig of rosemary

3 hot Italian sausages (4 oz/110g each)

3 sweet Italian sausages (4 oz/110g each)

3 tablespoons olive oil

1 pound/450g fresh tagliatelle

3 plum tomatoes, cut into ¼-inch/0.5-cm dice, juice reserved

¾ cup/170ml heavy cream

2 tablespoons unsalted butter

¼ cup/55g defrosted frozen peas or blanched fresh peas

¾ cup/85g freshly grated Parmigiano-Reggiano

Bring a large pot of salted water to a boil.

While the water is boiling, chop the sage and rosemary together into a thick paste. Reserve. Remove the casings from all the sausages and knead them together by hand.

Warm the olive oil in a sauté pan wide and deep enough to hold all the ingredients over medium heat. Add the sausage in small batches and cook until browned, about 5 minutes. As the sausage cooks, use a spatula to break up the meat until it looks like ground beef.

Add the tagliatelle to the boiling water and cook until done, 2 to 3 minutes.

Add the tomatoes and the sage-rosemary mixture to the sausages. Stir and cook for 2 minutes. Add the cream, butter, peas, and Parmigiano. Stir and cook for 1 minute, just to warm the ingredients.

Drain the pasta and immediately add it to the pan with the sauce. Toss well.

Serve family-style from a large serving bowl, or divide among individual bowls. Grind pepper over the pasta at the table.

WINE SUGGESTION: **"I Sodi di San Niccolò"**–*Castellare di Castellina*

penne strasciate

DRAGGED PASTA

This is my favorite meat sauce, so I've provided a recipe that makes an enormous quantity. Use 2 to 3 cups with one pound of penne the first night, and store the rest in the refrigerator or freezer and use it as your "house" pasta sauce.

Strasciate means "dragged", and it's essential that you drag the penne through this sauce. It's a thin sauce, but it will adhere to the pasta.

makes about 5 quarts/5 litres sauce, enough for about 20 servings serves 4 to 6 (the first night)

10 tablespoons olive oil

3¼ pounds/1.5kg ground beef

3½ pounds/1.6kg ground veal

2 pounds/900g ground pork

2 pounds/900g chicken livers, roughly chopped

Fine sea salt

Freshly ground black pepper

4 celery stalks, roughly chopped

2 large carrots or 4 small carrots, peeled and roughly chopped

2 medium red onions, roughly chopped

1 cup/220ml dry red wine

10 tablespoons tomato paste

2 bay leaves

½ cup/110ml milk

1 pound/450g penne

¼ cup/30g freshly grated Parmigiano-Reggiano

1 teaspoon unsalted butter

Warm 5 tablespoons of the olive oil in a large pot over medium-high heat. Add the beef, veal, pork, and chicken livers in small increments, season with salt and pepper, and cook until uniformly browned, about 15 minutes. Drain any excess liquid from the pot and turn off the heat.

In a sauté pan, warm the remaining 5 tablespoons olive oil over medium heat. Add the celery, carrots, and onions and cook until the onions color, about 7 minutes. Transfer the vegetables to the pot with the meat and place the pot over high heat.

Add the wine and stir. Add the tomato paste, stir, and cover with water by 1 inch/2.5cm. Season well with salt and pepper, add the bay leaves, and stir again. When the mixture comes to a boil, lower the heat and let the sauce simmer for 4 hours.

About 15 minutes before serving, bring a large pot of salted water to a boil.

Fish the bay leaves out of the sauce and discard them. Stir in the milk.

Add the penne to the boiling water, cover to return to the boil, then cook, uncovered, until al dente, about 10 minutes. Drain the pasta and transfer it to a sauté pan. Add 2 to 3 cups of the sauce to the pan, stir in the butter, sprinkle with the cheese and sauté over medium heat for 2 minutes. Divide among individual bowls or serve from a large family-style bowl.

Allow the remaining sauce to cool, then refrigerate it in small, airtight containers for up to 1 week, or freeze for up to 2 months.

WINE SUGGESTION: **Barolo, "La Serra"–Marcarini**

risotto ai carciofi

ARTICHOKE RISOTTO

You'll taste artichoke in every bite of this risotto because, by cooking the artichokes in the pot before adding the rice and stock, the entire dish becomes infused with their flavor. I don't recommend doing this with most vegetables (usually I cook them separately and add them at the end), but artichokes are sturdy enough to be cooked for twenty minutes without losing their character.

serves 4 to 6

1 lemon, halved

8 baby artichokes

2 quarts/2 litres Brodo di Carne (page 183), canned low-sodium beef broth, or chicken or vegetable stock

5 tablespoons olive oil

1 leek, white part only, well washed and minced

1 clove garlic, minced

1 pound/450g (2 cups) Carnaroli or Arborio rice

½ cup/110ml dry white wine

1 tablespoon unsalted butter

1 cup/110g freshly grated Parmigiano-Reggiano

Fine sea salt

Freshly ground black pepper

Fill a stainless steel or ceramic bowl large enough to hold the artichokes with cold water. Squeeze the juice from the lemon halves into the bowl. Clean and trim the artichokes down to the heart by cutting off the stems and snapping back and removing all the tough outer leaves. Quarter the hearts and place them in the bowl with the lemon water to keep them from discoloring.

Pour the brodo into a pot and bring it to a simmer over high heat. Lower the heat and allow the stock to simmer.

Warm the olive oil in a heavy-bottomed pot large enough to hold all the ingredients over medium heat. Add the leek and garlic and sauté for 3 minutes.

While the leek and garlic are cooking, drain the artichoke hearts and pat them dry with paper towels. Add the artichoke hearts to the leek and garlic and cook until the artichoke hearts begin to color, about 5 minutes. Add the rice and stir to coat it with oil. Fry the rice, stirring constantly, until it turns opaque in the center, 3 to 4 minutes. Add the wine and stir until it evaporates, about 1 minute.

Add about 1 cup/225ml of the simmering stock and cook, stirring constantly, until the rice is almost dry. Continue to add stock by the ladleful, stirring as you cook and adding more stock only as the previous addition has been absorbed. After about 15 minutes, begin adding the stock in smaller increments until you reach the desired consistency, with the rice fully cooked but still a bit al dente and with a slightly creamy consistency.

Just before serving, add the butter and Parmigiano, season with salt and pepper, and stir vigorously until the risotto is creamy. Serve family-style from a large serving bowl or divide among individual bowls.

WINE SUGGESTION: **"Dreams"–Jermann**

RISOtto aLLe VONGOLe

RISOTTO WITH CLAMS

This is my version of risotto with clams. Don't worry about keeping the cooked clams warm; they'll reheat in the risotto at the end.

SERVES 4 to 6

10 tablespoons olive oil

2 cloves garlic, crushed and peeled

50 small clams, preferably from New Zealand

¼ teaspoon crushed red pepper

2 tablespoons minced flat-leaf parsley leaves

1 cup/220ml dry white wine

2 quarts/2 litres Brodo di Verdure (page 185), canned low-sodium vegetable stock, or chicken stock

1 leek, white part only, well washed and minced

1 clove garlic, minced

1 pound/450g (2 cups) Carnaroli or Arborio rice

Fine sea salt to taste

Freshly ground black pepper

Warm 4 tablespoons of the olive oil in a pan wide and deep enough to hold the clams over medium heat. Add the crushed garlic cloves and cook until they brown, about 5 minutes. Add the clams, red pepper, and parsley. Cook, covered, until the clams open, 4 to 5 minutes.

Pour ½ cup/110ml of the wine over the open clams, then turn off the heat. Use tongs to discard any clams that have not opened. As soon as they are cool enough to handle, remove the clams from their shells. Reserve.

Pour the brodo into a pot and bring it to a simmer over high heat. Lower the heat and allow the stock to simmer.

Warm the remaining olive oil in a heavy-bottomed pot large enough to hold all the ingredients over medium heat. Add the leek and minced garlic and sauté for 3 minutes. Add the rice and stir to coat with oil. Fry the rice, stirring constantly, until it turns opaque in the center, 3 to 4 minutes. Add the remaining ½ cup/110ml of wine and stir until it evaporates, about 1 minute.

Add about 1 cup/225ml of the simmering stock to the pot and cook, stirring constantly, until the rice is almost dry. Continue to add stock by the ladleful, stirring as you cook and adding more stock only as the previous addition has been absorbed. After about 15 minutes, begin adding the stock in smaller increments until you reach the desired consistency, with the rice fully cooked but still a bit al dente and with a slightly creamy consistency.

Just before serving, fold the clams into the risotto, season with salt and pepper, and stir gently.

Serve family-style from a large serving bowl, or divide among individual bowls.

WINE SUGGESTION: **Arneis, "Blangé"–Ceretto**

risotto alla milanese

MILAN-STYLE RISOTTO

This dish exists for one reason—to provide the perfect accompaniment to Osso Buco *alla Milanese* (page 139), though you could eat it on its own. The saffron threads turn the risotto a beautiful bright yellow.

serves 4 to 6

2 quarts/2 litres Brodo di Verdure (page 185), canned low-sodium vegetable stock, or chicken stock

½ teaspoon saffron threads

¼ cup/55ml olive oil

1 white onion, cut into ¼-inch dice

1 pound/450g (2 cups) Carnaroli or Arborio rice

½ cup/110ml dry white wine

Fine sea salt to taste

Freshly ground black pepper

1 tablespoon unsalted butter

1 cup/220ml heavy cream

½ cup/55g freshly grated Parmigiano-Reggiano

Pour the brodo into a pot and bring it to a boil over high heat. Lower the heat and allow the stock to simmer.

Place the saffron threads in a small ceramic or stainless steel bowl and ladle a few tablespoons of hot stock over them. Allow to soak as you proceed with the risotto.

Warm the olive oil in a heavy-bottomed pot large enough to hold all the ingredients over medium heat. Add the onion and sauté for 3 minutes. Add the rice and stir to coat it with oil. Fry the rice, stirring constantly, until it turns opaque in the center, 3 to 4 minutes. Add the wine and stir until it evaporates, about 1 minute.

Add about 1 cup/225ml of the simmering stock and cook, stirring constantly, until the rice is almost dry. Continue to add stock by the ladleful, stirring as you cook and adding more stock only as the previous addition has been absorbed. After about 8 minutes, add the saffron threads and their soaking liquid to the pot and continue. After about 15 minutes, begin adding the stock in smaller increments until you reach the desired consistency, with the rice fully cooked but still a bit al dente and with a slightly creamy consistency.

Just before serving, season the risotto with salt and pepper, fold in the butter, cream, and Parmigiano, and stir vigorously.

Serve family-style from a large serving bowl, or divide among individual bowls.

pappa al pomodoro

TOMATO AND BREAD SOUP

This hearty soup is Italian comfort food if there ever was such a thing. It's also my girlfriend's favorite soup, so we eat it at home as much as we do at Da Silvano.

makes about 2 quarts/2 litres, 6 to 8 servings

5 tablespoons olive oil

1 medium red onion, roughly chopped

1 quart/1 litre Brodo di Verdure (page 185) or canned low-sodium vegetable broth

4 pounds/1.8kg very ripe plum tomatoes, peeled and cut into 1-inch cubes, seeds and liquid reserved (see Sidebar)

Fine sea salt

Freshly ground black pepper

¼ loaf day-old country bread, crusts removed, cut into 1-inch/2.5-cm cubes (about 8 cups/225g bread cubes)

8 to 16 basil leaves, for garnish

Warm 4 tablespoons of the olive oil in a pot large enough to hold all of the ingredients over medium heat. Add the onion and cook until golden brown, about 5 minutes. Add the brodo and the tomatoes, along with their seeds and liquid. Season with salt and pepper. Raise the heat to high and bring the liquid to a boil. Lower the heat and cook at a simmer until the tomatoes break down and the soup begins to thicken, 30 to 40 minutes. Add the bread cubes and cook, stirring to break them down, for 15 to 20 minutes.

Serve the soup in individual bowls, hot or at room temperature, garnishing each serving with a few grinds of black pepper, a drizzle of olive oil, and a basil leaf or two.

How to Peel Tomatoes

First fill a bowl with ice water and set it aside. Bring a large pot of salted water to a boil over high heat. While the water is boiling, prepare the tomatoes: Use a very sharp paring knife to slice a shallow X just deep enough to pierce the skin across the bottom and cut a small hole at the top of the tomato, where the stem has been removed. When the water reaches a boil, carefully lower the tomatoes into the water and cook until the skin begins to pull away from the tomatoes, about 1 minute. Use tongs or a slotted spoon to remove the tomatoes from the boiling water and plunge them in the ice water. As soon as they've cooled, remove the skin, which should come right off with the aid of a paring knife.

WINE SUGGESTION: **Vino Nobile di Montepulciano–Bortoluzzi**

minestrone aLLa toscana

TUSCAN VEGETABLE SOUP

This soup takes me back to my Florentine youth, when I would come home after playing in the streets all morning and my mother would have a pot of it on the stove for me.

If you've ever wondered why there are so many soups that go by the name minestrone, it's because the name just means vegetable soup. There are almost as many variations as there are cooks.

makes about 2 quarts/2 litres, 6 to 8 servings

8 ounces/225g (1 cup) dried cannellini beans

Fine sea salt

1 medium red onion, quartered with roots attached

3 tablespoons olive oil

1 medium red onion, roughly chopped

3 medium Yukon Gold potatoes

3 tablespoons tomato paste

2 celery stalks, cut crosswise into ¼-inch/0.5-cm slices

2 large carrots, cut into ¼-inch/0.5-cm rounds

1 Savoy cabbage (about 2 lb/900g), core removed and discarded, coarsely chopped

1 cup/100g defrosted frozen peas or blanched fresh peas

Soak the cannellini beans overnight in enough cold water to cover. Drain.

Bring 2 quarts/2 litres of lightly salted water to a boil over high heat. Add the beans and the quartered onion. Bring back to the boil, then lower the heat and let simmer until the beans are cooked, about 1 hour.

Drain the beans over a bowl. Reserve the beans and their cooking liquid separately. When the beans are cool enough to handle, pick out and discard the onion.

Peel the potatoes. Cut two of them into 1-inch/2.5-cm slices, then cut each slice into quarters. Leave the third potato whole.

Warm the olive oil in a large pot over medium heat. Add the chopped onion and sauté until lightly colored, about 7 minutes. Add the potato slices and sauté until they begin to color, about 5 minutes. Add the tomato paste and stir to coat the potatoes with the paste. Cook for 3 minutes. Add the celery, carrots, cabbage, beans, and the whole potato.

Freshly ground black pepper

Extra virgin olive oil, for drizzling (optional)

Add the bean cooking liquid to the pot, plus enough water to cover by 1 inch/2.5 cm. Raise the heat to high and bring the water to a boil. Lower the heat immediately and cook until the whole potato is cooked through, about 15 minutes. Test for doneness by inserting a sharp, thin-bladed knife into the potato. Remove the whole potato, mash or rice it, and return it to the pot, stirring it in to thicken the soup. Stir the peas into the soup. Season with salt and pepper.

Divide among individual bowls and, if desired, drizzle some extra virgin olive oil over each serving.

WINE SUGGESTION: **Morellino di Scassino–Constantia**

zuppa di funghi

When porcini are in season, I eat them as much as possible. They're delicious sautéed on their own, but they're also quite expensive. This soup is a good way to get the most out of porcini without using too many of them.

makes about 2 quarts/2 litres, 6 to 8 servings

2 quarts/2 litres **Brodo di Carne** (page 183) or canned low-sodium beef broth

2 fresh porcini mushrooms, cleaned and thinly sliced

2 medium vine-ripened tomatoes, each cut into 8 slices

Fine sea salt

Freshly ground black pepper

6 tablespoons minced flat-leaf parsley

Extra virgin olive oil, for drizzling (optional)

Bring the brodo to a boil in a pot large enough to hold all ingredients over high heat. Lower the heat to medium, add the mushrooms and tomatoes and cook until the mushrooms are cooked through and their flavor has infused the broth, about 10 minutes. The tomatoes will disappear during this time. Season the soup with salt and pepper.

Divide among individual bowls, sprinkle each with minced parsley and, if desired, drizzle with olive oil.

80 DA SILVANO COOKBOOK

gazpacho modo mio

GAZPACHO, MY WAY

Gazpacho might sound Italian, but it's actually a Spanish soup. As is the case with so many Italian dishes, the Spanish have endless regional versions of gazpacho. They all have two things in common: bread and almonds. I don't use either. My take on gazpacho showcases the finely cut vegetables, the peppery kick, and the way this cools you down in the summer.

5 vine-ripened tomatoes, finely diced

4 scallions, white parts only, thinly sliced

2 small cucumbers, peeled and finely diced

1 red onion, peeled and finely diced

1 red pepper, seeds, stems, and ribs removed and finely diced

Fine sea salt

Freshly ground black pepper

1 quart/1 litre tomato juice or V-8

2 tablespoons olive oil

Splash of red wine vinegar

¼ teaspoon Tabasco sauce, or more to taste

makes about 2 quarts/2 litres, 4 to 6 servings

Place the tomatoes, scallions, cucumbers, onion, and red pepper in a large mixing bowl. Season with salt and pepper and gently toss. Pour the tomato juice over the vegetables.

Ladle 1 quart/1 litre of this mixture into a blender and blend for 10 seconds, being careful not to liquefy it completely. (You may need to do this in batches.)

Return the blended soup to the bowl. Stir in the olive oil and vinegar. Add Tabasco to taste. Refrigerate for at least 1 hour and serve cold.

ZUPPA DI faRRO

This soup is the perfect way to warm up on a cold winter day. This won't become clear until you add the sage-infused oil at the very end—it changes the character of the entire soup.

Use exactly as much water as the recipe says to cook the beans; it takes on the flavor of the beans, becoming the stock for the soup, and you don't want it to become diluted. Since the water is the stock, you might want to cook the beans in bottled or purified water.

This soup is very thick, almost like a porridge. If you prefer a thinner soup, add some water, vegetable stock, or chicken stock.

makes about 2 quarts/2 litres, 6 to 8 servings

4 ounces/110g (½ cup) dried cranberry beans

4 ounces/110g (½ cup) dried cannellini beans

¾ pound/385g (1¾ cups) farro

3 large carrots, peeled and cut into 3 pieces each

3 medium red onions, peeled and quartered with roots attached

3 celery stalks, cut into 3 pieces each

16 sage leaves

Fine sea salt

Freshly ground black pepper

Water, chicken stock, or vegetable stock (optional)

Soak the cranberry beans, the cannellini beans, and farro overnight in separate bowls in enough cold water to cover them. When ready to prepare the soup, drain all three and rinse the farro in several changes of cold water to remove any grit.

Put the cranberry beans, cannellini beans, and farro in separate pots. Add 2 quarts/2 litres of water, 3 carrot pieces, 4 onion quarters, 3 celery pieces, and 4 sage leaves to each pot. Reserve the remaining 4 sage leaves. Season the water in each pot with salt and pepper. Place each pot over high heat and bring to a boil. Lower the heat and let simmer until done, 45 minutes to 1 hour.

Set a fine mesh strainer over a bowl and drain the cranberry beans and cannellini beans through it. Reserve the liquid and the beans separately. Drain the farro over the sink, discarding the cooking liquid. Use tongs to remove and discard the carrot, onion, and celery from the beans and farro.

5 tablespoons olive oil

4 cloves garlic, smashed and peeled

Extra virgin olive oil, for drizzling (optional)

Transfer the beans to a food processor and purée until the texture is uniformly smooth and creamy.

Transfer the bean purée, drained farro, and 3½ cups/387.5ml of the reserved bean-cooking liquid to a large pot. Set the pot over low heat and cook, stirring to incorporate the ingredients. If the soup seems too thick, add more cooking liquid. Leave over low heat while you prepare the sage oil.

Pour the olive oil into a small sauté pan and warm it over medium heat. When the oil is hot, but not smoking, add the garlic and cook until golden brown, 3 to 4 minutes. Add the reserved 4 sage leaves to the pan, swirl, and let cook for a few seconds only. Pour the oil into the soup and stir it in. Taste the soup and adjust the seasoning if necessary.

Divide the soup among individual bowls. If you like, drizzle each serving with a little extra virgin olive oil.

WINE SUGGESTION: **Casalferro–Barone Ricasoli**

zuppa all' aglio

Nick Tosches loves this dish. In fact, Nick loves almost anything with garlic in it. He is always my first customer of the day for lunch, and I try to have this soup on hand for him.

The first step is going to take you a lot of time, but once you've done it the rest is easy. First, peel the cloves of 8 heads of garlic. Discard any cloves with green shoots as they will ruin the delicate taste of this soup.

8 heads of garlic

6 tablespoons olive oil

1 leek, white part only, well washed and finely chopped

2 medium baking potatoes, peeled and cut into medium dice

Fine sea salt

Freshly ground black pepper

2 quarts/2 litres Brodo di Carne (page 183) or canned low-sodium beef broth

makes about 2 quarts/2 litres, 6 to 8 servings

Separate the garlic heads into cloves, smash each clove, and discard the skin. Set aside.

Warm the olive oil in a pot over medium heat. Add the leek and cook until lightly colored, about 6 minutes. Add the potato and garlic, season with salt and pepper, and cook for 5 minutes. Add the broth, raise the heat, and bring the broth to a boil. Lower the heat, cover the pot, and let the soup simmer until the garlic falls apart with the touch of a wooden spoon, 1½ to 2 hours.

Carefully purée the soup in a food processor, or use a blender, being very careful of the hot liquid. Blend to a pleasing, creamy texture. (You can also use an immersion blender.)

WINE SUGGESTION: **Morellino di Scansano–Belguardo**

zuppa alla porcara

The combination of broccoli di rapa and sausage dominates this soup, but the other vegetables add valuable flavors and textures. The cheese here isn't just an afterthought; it really pulls the soup together at the last second.

makes about 2 quarts/2 litres, 6 to 8 servings

5 tablespoons olive oil

1 medium red onion, cut into ¼-inch/0.5-cm dice

1 small Yukon Gold potato, scrubbed, cut into 1-inch/2.5-cm slices, each slice cut in half

1 leek, white part only, well washed and roughly chopped

1 pound/450g broccoli di rapa, roughly chopped

2 pounds/900g Swiss chard, tough stems trimmed and discarded, leaves roughly chopped

Fine sea salt

Freshly ground black pepper

1 to 2 sweet Italian sausages (about 4 oz/110g total), casings removed and cut into ½-inch/1-cm-thick slices

¼ cup/30g freshly grated Parmigiano-Reggiano

Warm 3 tablespoons of the olive oil in a large pot over medium heat. Add the onion and cook until lightly colored, about 7 minutes. Add the potato and cook for 2 minutes. Add the leek, broccoli di rapa, and Swiss chard. Season with salt and pepper, stir, and cover with water by 1 inch/2.5 cm. Raise the heat to high and bring the soup to a boil.

While the soup is coming to a boil, warm the remaining 2 tablespoons olive oil in a sauté pan set over medium-high heat. Add the sausage slices to the sauté pan. When the soup reaches a boil, lower the heat to let it simmer.

Cook the sausage slices in a sauté pan over medium heat until browned and cooked through, 5 to 7 minutes. Use a slotted spoon or tongs to add the sausages to the soup, leaving the grease behind in the sauté pan. Cook the soup at a simmer for 45 minutes. Season the soup with salt and pepper.

Divide the soup among individual bowls and sprinkle some cheese over each serving.

WINE SUGGESTION: **Morellino di Scansano–Costantia**

pasta e fagioli

Pasta and bean soup is a classic Italian dish that's extremely substantial and satisfying. It's warming and comforting during the cooler times of the year—late fall through early spring—because it takes the chill right out of you. But I like the flavors so much that I also eat it at room temperature in the summer. If you choose to do the same, skip the step of puréeing a portion of the soup and add a little extra broth instead; it will be better cold if it's thinner.

If you won't be eating this at once, leave out the pasta and add it when you reheat the soup so it doesn't become soggy.

makes about 2 quarts/2 litres, 6 to 8 servings

1 pound/450g (2 cups) dried cannellini beans

Fine sea salt

¼ cup olive oil

4 garlic cloves, crushed and peeled

1 medium red onion, peeled and cut into ¼-inch/0.5cm dice

2 cups/450g *Sugo di Pomodoro* (page 182)

4 cups/900ml *Brodo di Carne* (page 183) or low-sodium canned beef broth

2 fresh sage leaves

Freshly ground black pepper

1 pound/450g fresh pappardelle, cut into 2-inch/5-cm pieces

Soak the beans overnight in enough cold water to cover. Drain.

Bring a large pot of salted water to a boil over high heat. Add the beans, lower the heat, and cook at a simmer for 1 hour, or until al dente. Drain the beans and reserve.

Warm the olive oil in a pot large enough to hold all the ingredients over medium heat. Add 2 garlic cloves and the diced onion to the pot. When the onion has colored slightly, about 5 minutes, remove the pot from the heat. Add the sugo, the beans, and the brodo.

Return the pot to the stovetop over high heat. Add the 2 remaining garlic cloves and 2 sage leaves. Season to taste with salt and pepper. As soon as the soup boils, lower the heat and let simmer for 10 minutes. Remove the pot from the heat. Ladle a fourth of the soup into a blender and purée it. Return the purée to the pot and stir to incorporate it into the soup and thicken it.

High-quality extra virgin olive oil, for drizzling (optional)

1 cup/110g freshly grated Parmigiano-Reggiano

6 to 8 sage leaves, to garnish the soup (1 leaf per bowl)

Place the pot over medium heat and add the pappardelle. Cook until the pasta is done, about 3 minutes.

Ladle the soup into bowls, top each with a few grinds of black pepper, drizzle with extra virgin olive oil (if desired), sprinkle with Parmigiano, and garnish each bowl with a sage leaf.

WINE SUGGESTION: **"Super Tuscan" Semifonte di Semifonte**

RIBOLLita

This is my version of a Tuscan standard. The ingredients break down during the long cooking time, and you're left with a thick, delicious soup. Because it keeps especially well (in fact, it needs to be made a day in advance), I've provided a recipe that yields a large quantity—save the extra for the next day, or freeze it for up to 2 weeks.

makes about 3 quarts/3 litres, 8 to 12 servings

8 ounces/225g (1 cup) dried cannellini beans

Fine sea salt

Freshly ground black pepper

2 cloves garlic, smashed and peeled

¾ cup to 1¼ cups/175-300ml olive oil

1 large red onion, roughly chopped

1 leek, white part only, well washed and roughly chopped

1 medium Yukon Gold potato, peeled and cut into ¼-inch/0.5-cm dice

20 leaves *cavolo nero*, minced (see Note)

½ Savoy cabbage (about 12 oz/350g), roughly chopped

1 medium zucchini, roughly chopped

2 celery stalks, roughly chopped

Soak the cannellini beans overnight in enough cold water to cover. Drain.

Transfer the beans to a pot, cover with cold water, season with salt and pepper, and add the garlic to the pot. Bring to a boil over high heat, then lower the heat and cook at a simmer until the beans are done, about 1 hour. Drain and reserve the beans.

Warm ¼ cup/55ml of the olive oil in a pot large enough to hold all the ingredients over medium heat. Add the onion and the leek and cook until lightly colored, about 7 minutes. Add the diced potato, season with salt and pepper, and cook for 2 to 3 minutes. Add the beans, *cavolo nero*, Savoy cabbage, zucchini, celery, carrots, whole potato, and tomatoes, if using. Stir. Add the brodo and season with salt and pepper. Raise the heat to high and bring the stock to a boil. Lower the heat and let simmer, covered, for 2 hours. During this time, the ingredients will fall apart.

Use a slotted spoon to remove the whole potato from the soup. Mash it with a fork and stir it back into the soup to thicken it. Set the soup aside to cool. Refrigerate it overnight.

The next day, warm the soup over low heat.

2 large carrots or 4 small carrots, cut into ⅛-inch/0.25-cm rounds

1 medium Yukon Gold potato, peeled and left whole

4 plum tomatoes, peeled (optional)

2 quarts/2 litres Brodo di Pollo (page 184) or low-sodium canned chicken broth

8 to 12 thick slices country or peasant bread, preferably day-old (1 slice per serving)

1 cup to 1½ cups/110-175g freshly grated Parmigiano-Reggiano (optional)

While the soup is heating up, warm ¼ cup of the remaining olive oil in a sauté pan over low heat. Add 4 bread slices to the pan and fry them in the oil for about 2 minutes on each side. Repeat with additional bread slices.

Place a bread slice in the bottom of each bowl and spoon some soup over each serving. Top with some Parmigiano, if desired.

NOTE: *Cavolo nero*, or black cabbage, is indigenous to Tuscany and very difficult to find in the United States. You can substitute 10 Swiss chard leaves or 30 *broccoli di rapa* leaves.

WINE SUGGESTION: **"La Fonte"–*Terrabianca***

pesce e frutti di mare

FISH AND SHELLFISH

New York City could not be more different from the coastal regions of Italy where I spent my childhood summers. Forte dei Marmi may have become a more modern region today than it was when I was growing up decades ago, but if you visit there, you can still enjoy many of the seafood dishes in this chapter, which are now the stuff of legend.

But we are lucky in New York City, too. There are so many great seafood purveyors that you can get an incredible variety of high-quality fish and shellfish. Among the Tuscan classics we've been able to recreate at Da Silvano are Cacciucco, a hearty stew featuring fish and shellfish; *Tegamone*, a baked fish dish that features many of the same creatures of the sea in a very different context; Calamari in Zimino, in which calamari are cooked in a mixture of their own ink and tomato; and *Merluzzo alla Livornese*, a tribute to the cooking style of Leghorn. We also serve whole-roasted fish, including red snapper and pompano.

Then there are those recipes that have been inspired by my travels elsewhere in Italy and around the world, including *Langostine alla Catalana*

and a variation featuring lobster; *Pesce Spada alla Veneziana*, a wonderful version of swordfish and onions; and *Spiedino di Pesce Riminese*, a mixed-seafood skewer that is great in the summertime.

Of course, living in New York for over twenty-five years, I've been very influenced by what New Yorkers find most appealing. There's no more popular fish in Manhattan than tuna, and I've included two tuna recipes, *Tonno Pepato*, based on the French steak *au poivre* I used to eat with great frequency in Paris, and the sushi-inspired *Tonno alla Tartara*, in the Italian style, with capers, anchovy, and olive oil.

Then there are those we made up at Da Silvano. I don't remember the day we created our *Insalata di Aragosta*, or lobster salad, but it's become one of our most popular dishes. I do remember the way I came up with the *Salmone Marinato Freddo*, or cold poached salmon; that story is on page 96.

There's really no end to what you can do with seafood. This chapter is just a sampling, but I hope there's enough variety to keep you coming back again and again the way my customers do at Da Silvano.

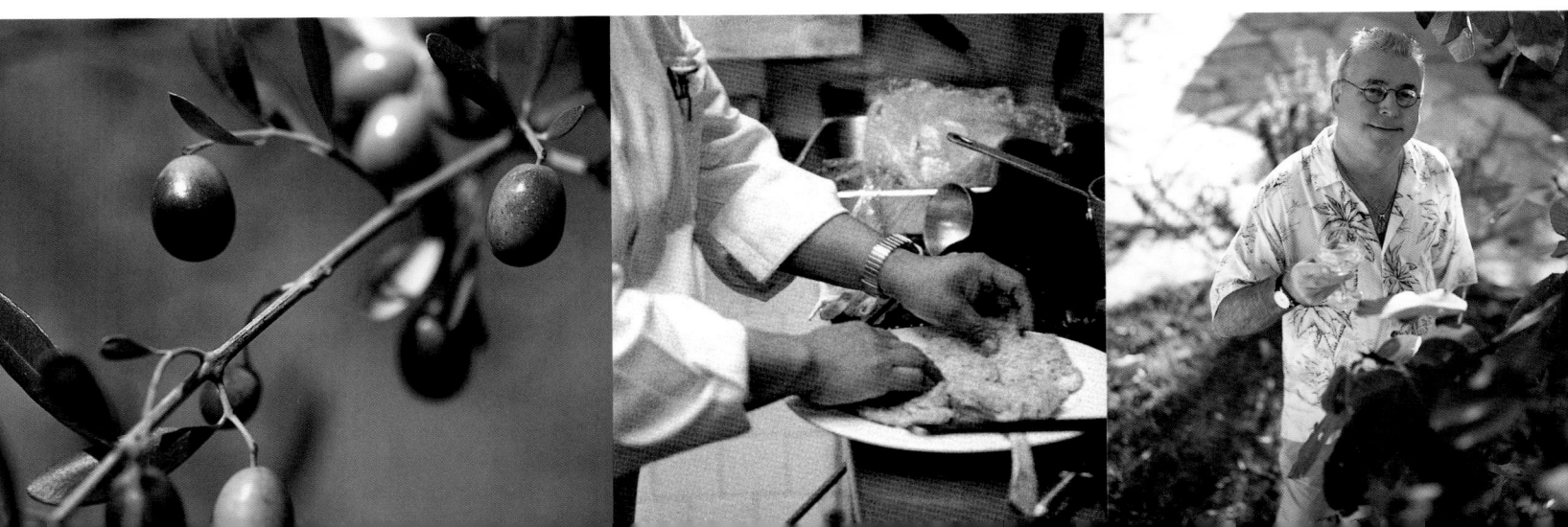

CODA DI ROSPO AI PORCINI

MONKFISH WITH PORCINI MUSHROOMS

Monkfish is very meaty, which makes it substantial enough to stand up to other strong ingredients, like porcini mushrooms. It also takes longer to cook than most fish, so I let it take on the flavor of the mushrooms and tomatoes during ten minutes of gentle steaming.

Serve this with *Spinaci* (page 154) or *Zucchini Trifolati* (page 158).

SERVES 4

4 skinless monkish fillets (about 8 oz/225g each)

Fine sea salt

Freshly ground black pepper

¼ cup/55ml olive oil

1 shallot, minced

8 ounces/225g fresh porcini mushrooms or 1 cup/30g dried porcini, reconstituted in warm water, thinly sliced (see Sidebar)

1 cup/225ml dry white wine

2 plum tomatoes, cut into ¼-inch/0.5-cm dice

1 tablespoon unsalted butter (optional)

4 sprigs of flat-leaf parsley

Season the monkfish fillets on both sides with salt and pepper. Warm the olive oil in a pan wide enough to hold the fish fillets without crowding over medium heat. Add the shallot and cook until lightly colored, 1 to 2 minutes. Add the fish, skinned-side down, to the pan and cook until browned, 2 to 3 minutes. Flip the fillets and cook until browned on the other side, 2 to 3 minutes more.

Add the mushrooms and wine to the pan and cook until the liquid has reduced by half, about 3 minutes. Scatter the diced tomato over the fish fillets and cover the pan with a lid.

Lower the heat to low and cook for 10 minutes.

Transfer the fish to a platter. If you would like to enrich the sauce, swirl in 1 tablespoon butter. Spoon some sauce over each fillet, making sure each spoonful includes some mushroom and tomato. Garnish each dish with a parsley sprig and serve.

How to Reconstitute Dried Porcini Mushrooms

Place the mushrooms in a ceramic or stainless-steel bowl, cover them with hot water, and let soak for 20 minutes. Drain and gently squeeze out any excess moisture. (Sometimes, the soaking liquid can be a powerful source of flavor, especially in soups and risotto, but it has no use here.)

WINE SUGGESTION: **Chardonnay, "Le Bruniche"–Nozzole**

salmone marinato freddo

Italians are very resourceful people when it comes to food, and I'm proud to say I'm no different. I made up this recipe when I showed up to stay for the night at a house in Stony Point, Long Island, and found that the gas had been shut off. I found some wood and a pot, started a fire, and made this dish.

Serve this with *Pomodori Reali* (page 160).

serves 4

Fine sea salt

1 large carrot, peeled and cut into ⅛-inch/0.25-cm rounds

1 medium red onion, peeled and quartered

1 celery stalk, cut into 3 large pieces

4 skin-on salmon fillets (about 8 oz/225g each)

8 cherry tomatoes, halved

¼ cup/55ml Pesto, without cheese (page 188)

½ cup/110ml Vinaigrette Modo Mio (page 186)

Bring a large pot of salted water to a boil over high heat. Add the carrot, onion, and celery, then carefully lower the salmon fillets into the pot, one at a time. Lower the heat and cook at a simmer until the salmon is cooked through but still firm, 5 to 7 minutes, depending on the thickness of the fillets. (If you prefer your fish rare, cook it a bit less.) If necessary, remove a fillet and cut into it with a paring knife to check for doneness. Keep in mind that it will continue to cook a bit by the retained heat after you take it out of the water.

Carefully remove the salmon fillets from the water and set aside to cool. Remove and discard the celery and onion. Drain the remaining liquid in a colander and refresh the carrots under gently running cold water. Cover the salmon and carrots separately and refrigerate them for at least 1 hour or up to 4 hours. Place 4 dinner plates in the refrigerator at the same time so they'll be chilled when you're ready to serve.

When ready to serve, remove the skin from each salmon fillet and cut each fillet into 4 equal portions. Place the pieces of 1 fillet in the center of each of the 4 chilled dinner plates, skinned-side down. Surround the fillets with the cherry tomato halves and carrot rounds. Pour the pesto and vinaigrette into a mixing bowl and stir them together. Drizzle some of the mixture over each portion of salmon and serve immediately, while still cold.

WINE SUGGESTION: **Sauvignon, "Graf de Latour"–Villa Russiz**

tonno alla tartara

TUNA TARTAR

Living in New York City, I've come to appreciate a lot of food that I never experienced in Italy. One of my favorites is sushi. This recipe uses Italian ingredients (capers, anchovies, olive oil), but was inspired by my love of raw tuna in sushi bars throughout Manhattan. Don't add the lemon juice until just before you're ready to serve, or it will turn the tuna brown.

I don't recommend any accompaniments here; enjoy this as a light lunch all by itself.

SERVES 4

2 tablespoons minced red onion

1 teaspoon capers, drained but not rinsed

2 anchovy fillets, minced

1 tablespoon minced flat-leaf parsley

2 pounds/900g sushi-grade tuna, well chilled

5 tablespoons olive oil

Juice of ½ a lemon

Fine sea salt

Freshly ground black pepper

8 slices white bread, crusts removed, toasted, and cut in half diagonally

Set 4 plates in the refrigerator to chill.

Place the onion, capers, anchovies, and parsley on a cutting board and chop them together. Transfer to a stainless steel bowl large enough to hold the tuna.

Cut the tuna into ¼-inch/0.5-cm cubes and add to the onion mixture.

Drizzle with the olive oil and gently toss. Add half of the lemon juice and gently toss. Taste and add more lemon juice until you like the level of acidity. Season with salt and pepper, being mindful that the anchovies are salty.

Divide the tuna tartar among the 4 chilled plates, place 4 toast triangles around each portion, and serve.

WINE SUGGESTION: **Tocai–Ronco del Gnemiz**

tonno pepato

When I worked in Paris years ago, one of my favorite dishes to eat was steak *au poivre*—steak coated in coarsely ground pepper before it's cooked. This dish is made the same way, but with tuna in place of steak. It was an instant success when I introduced it at Da Silvano almost two decades ago, and it's still popular today.

Serve this with accompaniments you might enjoy with a steak, such as *Cime di Rapa* (page 163), *Spinaci* (page 154), or even *Purè di Patate* (page 164).

SERVES 4

4 sushi-grade tuna fillets (8 oz/225g each), each cut 6 inches/15 cm long and 2 inches/5 cm thick

½ cup/110ml olive oil

Fine sea salt

½ cup/55g coarsely ground black pepper or crushed black pepper

Juice of 1 lemon

Lightly coat each tuna fillet with 1 tablespoon olive oil, using your fingers to spread it out evenly. Season the tuna fillets lightly with salt. Spread the pepper out on a clean dry surface and roll the tuna fillets in the pepper, pressing down to make sure that it adheres to the fish.

Warm the remaining olive oil in a pan large enough to hold the tuna over medium-high heat. When the oil is hot, add the tuna fillets. Sear on all sides, about 90 seconds for each of 4 sides or longer for more well done.

Remove the tuna from the pan, slice each fillet into ¾-inch slices, divide among 4 dinner plates, drizzle with the lemon juice, and serve at once.

WINE SUGGESTION: **Fiano di Avellino–Feudi San Gregorio**

merLuzzo aLLa Livornese

This recipe is based on my very fond memories of seafood in Livorno (Leghorn in English). A lot of people make the dish with olives, but the original, authentic way is without them. As you can see, this way, there's nothing to distract you from the flavor of the cod.

Serve this with *Spinaci* (page 154), *Cime di Rapa* (page 163), or *Pomodori Reali* (page 160).

SERVES 4

1 cup/140g all-purpose flour

Fine sea salt

Freshly ground black pepper

4 skinless fresh cod fillets (about 8 oz/225g each)

¼ cup/55ml vegetable oil, such as soybean or canola

¼ cup/55ml olive oil

4 cloves garlic, smashed and peeled

¼ teaspoon crushed red pepper

4 fresh plum tomatoes, quartered

3 tablespoons minced flat-leaf parsley

Spread the flour out on a clean, dry surface and season it with salt and pepper. Press both sides of the fillets into the flour. Reserve.

Warm the vegetable oil in a pan wide and deep enough to hold the fish without crowding over high heat. Add the fish, skinned-side down, and cook until browned on the bottom, about 3 minutes. Flip and cook until browned on the other side, about 3 minutes more. Transfer the fish to paper towels to drain.

Warm the olive oil in a pan wide and deep enough to hold all the ingredients over medium heat. Add the garlic and red pepper to the pan, stir, and cook until the garlic has colored slightly, about 2 minutes. Add the tomatoes and cook for 1 minute. Add the fish, lower the heat to low, and cook until cooked through, 8 to 10 minutes.

Transfer the fish to a serving platter, and spoon some sauce over each fillet. Top with minced parsley and serve immediately.

WINE SUGGESTION: **Greco di Tufo–Feudi San Gregorio**

baccaLà aLLa vicentina

SALT COD WITH CREAM AND ONIONS

It's very unusual to find fish and cheese on the same plate anywhere in Italy, but it works here because of the unique flavor and texture of salt cod. Be sure to plan ahead to soak the cod and get the salt out or this dish will dehydrate you.

This is delicious with *Fiori di Zucca Fritti* (page 159) or *Bietola* (page 166).

serves 4

4 salt cod fillets (8 oz/225g each)

1 cup/140g all-purpose flour

Fine sea salt

Freshly ground black pepper

¼ cup/55ml vegetable oil, such as soybean or canola

5 tablespoons olive oil, or less

4 medium red onions, halved through the root and thinly sliced

1 cup/225ml heavy cream

1 cup/225ml whole milk

½ cup/55g freshly grated Parmigiano-Reggiano

4 anchovy fillets

Place the salt cod fillets in a ceramic or stainless steel bowl and cover with cold water. Cover and refrigerate for 3 days, changing the water every 24 hours. When ready to proceed, drain and pat the cod dry with paper towels.

Preheat the oven to 300°F/150°C/gas 2.

Spread the flour out on a clean, dry surface and season it with salt and pepper. Press both sides of the fillets into the flour. Reserve.

Warm the vegetable oil in a pan wide and deep enough to hold the fish without crowding over high heat. Add the fish, skinned-side down, and cook until browned on the bottom, about 3 minutes. Flip and cook until browned on the other side, about 3 minutes more. Transfer the fish to paper towels to drain.

Pour just enough olive oil into a casserole large enough to hold the fish fillets in a single layer without crowding to cover the bottom. Place the casserole over medium heat and warm the olive oil. Add the onions and cook until lightly colored, about 7 minutes. Spread the onions out over the bottom of the casserole and place the fish on top of them in a single layer. Pour the cream and milk over the fish and top with the cheese. Place 1 anchovy fillet on top of each cod fillet.

Cover the casserole with aluminum foil and bake for 15 minutes. Remove the foil and cook for 5 to 7 minutes more to brown the cheese.

Remove the casserole from the oven. Use a spatula to transfer 1 fillet to each of 4 dinner plates and serve immediately.

WINE SUGGESTION: **Greco di Tufi or Pinot Grigio**

dentice arrosto

Whole roasted fish are a staple at Italian restaurants, and Da Silvano is no different. Snapper is one of the most popular fish we serve. It resembles *dentice*, a Mediterranean fish, and it's especially beautiful when presented whole at the table.

Serve this with *Melanzane alla Griglia* (page 155), *Cime di Rapa* (page 163), or a simple mixed salad.

SERVES 4

1 whole red snapper, cleaned and gutted (about 2 lb/900g)

Fine sea salt

Freshly ground black pepper

2 cloves garlic, thinly sliced

1 sprig of rosemary

2 to 3 tablespoons olive oil

1 lemon, halved

Preheat the oven to 350°F/180°C/gas 4.

Season the cavity of the snapper with salt and pepper. Scatter the garlic inside the cavity and place the rosemary sprig inside.

Using a razor blade or a very sharp, very thin-bladed knife, score the fish at 1-inch/2.5-cm intervals on both sides. Drizzle about ½ tablespoon olive oil over each side of the fish and use your fingers to spread it out evenly. Season the fish on both sides with salt and pepper. Place the snapper on a baking sheet.

Bake for about 10 minutes per 1 inch/2.5 cm of fish (at its thickest part), probably about 30 minutes. Check on the fish after 20 minutes to be sure it isn't cooking too fast. Once the fish is cooked through, remove the baking sheet from the oven.

Transfer the fish to a platter, drizzle olive oil and squeeze some lemon juice over it, and serve whole, filleting it at the table.

WINE SUGGESTION: **Chardonnay from Tuscany or Greco di Tufo from Campania**

WHOLE-ROASTED POMPANO

For a variation on this dish, prepare 2 whole pompano (1 to 1½ lb/450 to 675g each) in the same manner, loosely wrapping the head and tail with aluminum foil.

caLamari in ZIMINO

SQUID WITH GREENS AND GARLIC

As popular as fried calamari is in the United States, when I introduce my American guests to this preparation, they never go back. It's not as crispy, but the flavor is far superior. Be sure to get some squid ink when you purchase the squid; it will turn your teeth black, but it's worth it.

serves 4

2 pounds/900g Swiss chard

¼ cup/55ml olive oil

4 scallions, white parts only, cut thinly crosswise

2 cloves garlic, minced

2 pounds/900g squid, cleaned and cut into ½-inch/1-cm rings

1 teaspoon crushed red pepper

Fine sea salt

Freshly ground black pepper

½ cup/110ml dry white wine

1 tablespoon calamari ink or double the amount of tomato paste

1 tablespoon tomato paste

Remove the stems of the Swiss chard, blanch the leaves, drain them, and pat dry. Cut the leaves crosswise into ½-inch/1-cm pieces. Set aside.

Warm the olive oil in a pan large enough to hold the squid over medium heat. Add the scallions and garlic and cook until lightly colored, 1 to 2 minutes. Add the squid and cook, stirring, for 30 seconds. Add the red pepper and Swiss chard and season with salt and pepper.

Add the wine, raise the heat to high, and cook until the wine has reduced almost completely, about 5 minutes. Lower the heat and add the squid ink and tomato paste. Cook over low heat until the sauce thickens and the squid is tender, 20 to 25 minutes.

Transfer to a large serving bowl and serve at once.

WINE SUGGESTION: **Franciacorta Cuvée–Ca' del Bosco or Bellavista**

SPIEDINO DI PESCE RIMINESE

SEAFOOD SKEWERS, INSPIRED BY RIMINI

This recipe is a tribute to my days as a cook at the Hotel Ambasciatori in Rimini. It can be served as a main course or a starter. You can prepare it indoors in a cast-iron pan, but I enjoy cooking and eating it outdoors and reminiscing about my days near the Adriatic Sea.

SERVES 4

1 red pepper, stem, seeds, and ribs removed and cut into 1-inch/2.5-cm pieces

1 yellow pepper, stem, seeds, and ribs removed and cut into 1-inch/2.5-cm pieces

3 tablespoons olive oil, plus more for oiling the grill grate

1⅓ cups/140g *Panata* (page 190)

1 pound/450g cleaned cuttlefish or squid, cut into 1-inch/2.5-cm rings

1 pound/450g swordfish, cut into 1-inch/2.5-cm cubes

1 pound/450g large shrimp, peeled, deveined, and cut into 1-inch/2.5-cm pieces

16 wooden skewers (8 inches/ 20 cm each), soaked in cold water

2 cups/115g salad greens

Prepare a fire in an outdoor grill and let it burn until covered with white ash.

Meanwhile, place the red and yellow pepper pieces in a small stainless steel or ceramic bowl and drizzle with the olive oil. Toss and reserve.

Spread the *panata* out on a clean, dry surface. Press the cuttlefish, swordfish, and shrimp pieces in the *panata* and coat on all sides.

Prepare the skewers by placing alternating pieces of seafood with 1 piece of red or yellow pepper after every 3 pieces of seafood on each skewer.

When the grill is ready, oil the grate. Place the skewers on the grill and cook 1 to 2 minutes on each of 4 sides.

Place ½ cup/30g salad greens on each of 4 plates and place 4 seafood skewers on top of each salad bed. Serve at once.

WINE SUGGESTION: **Sauvignon–Ronco del Gelso**

Langostine alla catalana

CATALAN-STYLE LANGOUSTINES

Langoustines are so beautiful and delicious that I believe in garnishing them with the simplest accompaniments. Here, they are simply split, sautéed, and covered with a mix of fresh vegetables. Most Americans I've met find the optional sauce too strong for this dish, but try it at least once; it's very delicious and easy to prepare (see Note).

SERVES 4

1 fennel bulb (about 12 oz/340g), hollow stalks removed and sliced (or shaved) thinly vertically

1 celery stalk, sliced crosswise as thin as possible

1 scallion, cleaned and left whole

8 plum tomatoes, cut into ¼-inch/0.5-cm dice

¾ cup/170ml olive oil

Fine sea salt

Freshly ground black pepper

12 langoustines, preferably from Iceland or New Zealand (about 3 oz/85g each)

Place the fennel, celery, scallion, and tomatoes in a stainless steel or ceramic mixing bowl, drizzle with ¼ cup/55ml of the olive oil, season with salt and pepper, and toss gently. Reserve.

Cut the langoustines lengthwise, leaving the shells intact.

Warm ¼ cup/55ml of the olive oil in each of 2 skillets large enough to hold half the langoustines over medium heat. When the oil is hot but not smoking, add the langoustines, open side down, to the pans. Cook for 1 minute, then flip and cook 1 minute more.

Remove the pans from the heat and transfer 3 langoustines to each of 4 plates. Top each serving with ¼ of the mixed vegetables. Serve at once.

NOTE: I top this dish with a simple sauce made by warming 5 tablespoons olive oil in a small sauté pan. Add an anchovy fillet and mash it with a spatula. Add a splash of lemon juice, remove the sauce from the heat, and spoon a little over each serving.

WINE SUGGESTION: **Vermentino–Santadi**

Lobster Alla Catalana

For a variation on this dish, place 1 live lobster (about 1¼ lb/560g) with its claws bound by rubber bands, 1 langoustine, and a handful of seaweed in a 1-gallon/3.8-litre plastic freezer bag. Squeeze a wedge of lemon into the bag, add the wedge to the bag, and seal the bag. Place in a microwave oven and cook on the highest setting for 10 minutes. Cut the bag open very carefully (it will be very hot and release a lot of steam). Cut the lobster and langoustine in half lengthwise, remove the sac behind the lobster's eyes and the tomalley from the lobster, and arrange them on a platter. Crack the lobster claws and place them on the platter. Scatter the vegetables over the seafood and serve immediately. At Da Silvano, this is a single portion though it is a lot of food, so cook as much as you require for you and your guests.

INSaLata DI aRagosta

LOBSTER SALAD

This is probably the most popular dish on the menu at Da Silvano. It could not be easier to prepare, but the flavors and textures are so rich (white Spanish beans, avocado, lemon juice, *rucola*, and—of course—lobster) that it makes quite an impact.

SERVES 4

¼ cup/30g dried white Spanish beans

Fine sea salt

Freshly ground black pepper

1 lemon, halved

4 lobsters (1 to 1½ lb/450 to 675g each)

1 avocado

1¼ cups/55g rucola

Juice of 1 lemon

2 tablespoons olive oil

2 tablespoons minced flat-leaf parsley

Soak the beans overnight in enough cold water to cover.

Drain the beans and transfer to a pot. Cover with cold water and season with salt and pepper. Bring to a boil over high heat, then lower the heat and cook the beans at a simmer until done, about 1 hour. Drain and reserve the beans.

Bring a stockpot full of water to a boil over high heat. Squeeze 2 lemon halves into the pot and carefully drop them into the water.

Add the lobsters to the pot and cook for 8 to 10 minutes.

Use tongs to remove the lobsters from the pot and let them cool.

When cool enough to handle, remove the meat from the lobster bodies and claws. Cut the meat into 1-inch/2.5-cm cubes. Reserve.

Cut the avocado in half lengthwise, remove the pit using the heel of a chef's knife, slice each half into 6 to 8 thin wedges, then remove the skin.

Arrange a bed of *rucola* on each of 4 salad plates. Arrange some beans on top of each bed and arrange 3 to 4 avocado wedges around the salad. Pile the lobster on top of the beans. Drizzle lemon juice and olive oil over each serving and top with minced parsley.

WINE SUGGESTION: **Franciacorta Brut–Bellavista**

pesce spada alla veneziana

VENETIAN-STYLE SWORDFISH

At the extraordinary Rialto market in Venice, they sell pristine cuts of swordfish referred to as *vitello di mare*, or veal of the sea. But even in the United States it's possible to find excellent swordfish that will shine in this simple recipe.

Serve this with *Spinaci* (page 154) or even *Purè di Patate* (page 164).

SERVES 4

¼ cup/55ml olive oil

2 medium red onions, halved through the root and thinly sliced

Fine sea salt

Freshly ground black pepper

2 pounds/900g skinless swordfish, cut into ¼-inch/ 0.5-cm-thick slices

Splash of dry white wine

Splash of red wine vinegar

3 tablespoons minced flat-leaf parsley

1 tablespoon unsalted butter

Divide the olive oil between 2 pans wide and deep enough to hold half the fish and half the onions. Warm over medium heat. Add half the onions to each pan, season with salt and pepper, and cook until lightly colored, about 7 minutes.

Season the swordfish slices on both sides with salt and pepper. Bank the onions to one side of each pan and add half the swordfish slices to each pan in a single layer as best you can. Raise the heat and cook the swordfish until warmed through, about 3 minutes on each side. Stir the swordfish and onions together. Reduce the heat to low and add a splash of white wine and red wine vinegar. Deglaze, then add half the parsley and half the butter to each pan. Stir and cook for 30 seconds.

Divide the swordfish and onions among 4 dinner plates and spoon some sauce over each serving.

WINE SUGGESTION: **Bátar–Az. Querciabella**

spiedini di scampi

This is a favorite dish of Victoria Sanders. Who's she? My neighbor. Celebrity or not, I really don't care. I'm flattered that so many superstars enjoy spending time in my restaurant, but I treat everyone the same. I always enjoy feeding people and seeing the pleasure they take in my food. If you don't believe me, drop in sometime.

SERVES 4

24 large shrimp, shelled, deveined, and cut into 1-inch/2.5-cm pieces

2 teaspoons minced flat-leaf parsley

½ teaspoon crushed red pepper

6 tablespoons olive oil

1 cup Panata (page 190)

Fine sea salt

Freshly ground black pepper

8 wooden skewers (8 inches/ 20 cm each), soaked in cold water

Juice of 1 lemon

Prepare an outdoor grill and let the coals burn until covered with white ash.

Place the shrimp pieces in a ceramic or stainless steel mixing bowl and toss with the parsley, red pepper, olive oil, and *panata*. Season with salt and pepper and toss again. Place the shrimp pieces on the skewers, pushing them together gently.

When the grill is ready, oil the grate. Place the shrimp skewers on the grill and cook for about 5 minutes on each side.

Remove from the heat, divide among 4 plates, and drizzle some lemon juice over each serving. Serve at once.

WINE SUGGESTION: **Terre di Tufi–Teruzzi & Puthod**

cacciucco

When I was a little boy, my family spent Sundays on the beach at Forte dei Marmi near Viareggio. One of my favorite memories of those days is of the local lifeguards who would cook cacciucco—a fish stew made mostly in seaport communities from fresh, local fish—in their homes and sell it to families like ours on the beach.

The types of seafood included change from town to town. This recipe uses my favorite combination, but you can also use gray mullet, shark, and other firm-fleshed fish. (In Italy, we always make cacciucco with scorfano, or scorpion fish, but it's very difficult to obtain in the United States, so I've left it out.)

serves 4

1¼ cups/300ml olive oil

8 cloves garlic, peeled and roughly chopped

1 large carrot, roughly chopped

1 small red onion, minced

½ teaspoon crushed red pepper

Fine sea salt

Freshly ground black pepper

¾ cup/40g minced flat-leaf parsley

1 pound/450g fresh cod, cut into 1-inch/2.5-cm cubes

1 cup/225ml dry white wine

½ cup/110ml white wine vinegar

4 cups/900g roughly chopped canned plum tomatoes (about 8 tomatoes)

Pour ½ cup/110ml of the olive oil into a pot large enough to hold all the ingredients and warm it over medium heat. Add the garlic, carrot, onion, and red pepper, season with salt and pepper, and cook, stirring occasionally, until the onion is lightly browned, about 7 minutes. Add ½ cup of the parsley and stir.

Add half the cod, along with the white wine, and cook until the wine reduces by two thirds, about 5 minutes. Add the vinegar and tomatoes, stir, and cook for 10 minutes. Add the remaining cod, the monkfish, scallops, bass, and swordfish. Season with salt and pepper and give a gentle stir. Then add the mussels and clams, letting them rest on top of the stew. Cover the pot and cook until the mussels and clams have opened, 5 to 10 minutes.

Meanwhile, warm ¼ cup/55ml of olive oil in a sauté pan over low heat. Add 4 bread slices and fry them in the oil for about 2 minutes on each side. Remove the bread slices and reserve. Repeat twice to use up the remaining olive oil and bread slices.

8 ounces/225g monkfish, cut into 1-inch/2.5cm cubes

1 cup/225g diver scallops

8 ounces/225g striped bass, cut into 1-inch/2.5cm cubes

8 ounces/225g swordfish, cut into 1-inch/2.5cm cubes

8 ounces/225g mussels, scrubbed and debearded

8 ounces/225g small clams, preferably from New Zealand

12 slices country or peasant bread

Ladle some *cacciucco* into each of 4 bowls and place a few clams and mussels on top of each serving. Sprinkle some of the remaining parsley over each serving. Serve each person 3 slices of fried bread.

WINE SUGGESTION: **Tocai–Plozner**

tegamone

BAKED FISH AND SHELLFISH

This dish is dedicated to my good friend Stefano from Florence, who makes a similar one in his restaurant in Galluzzo.

If you like, serve fried bread on the side, prepared the same way it is for *Cacciucco* (page 116).

5 tablespoons olive oil

4 cloves garlic, smashed and peeled

4 scallions, white parts only, minced

½ teaspoon crushed red pepper

16 mussels, cleaned and debearded

8 small clams

4 large shrimp or langoustines, peeled, deveined, and halved lengthwise

4 diver scallops

8 ounces/225g skinless swordfish, cut into 1-inch/ 2.5-cm cubes

Fine sea salt

Freshly ground black pepper

8 cherry tomatoes, crushed by hand

½ cup/110ml white wine

3 tablespoons minced flat-leaf parsley

Preheat the oven to 350°F/180°C/gas 4.

Warm the olive oil in a large, ovenproof sauté pan with sides at least 2 inches/5 cm high over medium heat. Add the garlic and scallions and cook until the garlic has colored slightly, 2 to 3 minutes. Add the red pepper, mussels, clams, shrimp, scallops, and swordfish and season with salt and pepper. Add the cherry tomatoes and white wine. Cook until the wine has reduced by half, about 2 minutes.

Transfer the pan to the oven and cook, uncovered, for 10 minutes.

Remove the pan from the oven and transfer the *tegamone* to a large serving bowl. Top with the parsley and serve immediately.

WINE SUGGESTION: **Chardonnay–Bortoluzzi**

118 DA SILVANO COOKBOOK

Beer, wines, and spirits play an important role in some of the dishes that follow. In the *Pollo alla Birra*, for example, we cook chicken in beer; in *Faraona al Barolo*, we cook guinea hen in rich, red wine; in *Coniglio in Casseurola*, rabbit benefits from the intensity of Cognac; and in *Anatra al Forno*, whole duck gets incredible flavor from vermouth.

Some of our most successful dishes are slow cooked, including my recipe for *Osso Buco alla Milanese*; *Stinco d'Agnello*, a variation on the same cooking technique, using lamb shanks; *Stracotto alla Fiorentina*, a long-cooked eye round of beef; and *Porchetta*, a whole-roasted pig that's great for large gatherings or holiday meals.

Of course, we also grill a lot of meat, including a lamb paillard, and the quintessential *Bistecca alla Fiorentina*—the ultimate example of how important the quality of your ingredients is. It features nothing but steak, olive oil, and lemon juice, but shop well and it's one of the best things you'll ever eat.

petto DI poLLo aL forno

BAKED BREADED CHICKEN BREAST

Sometimes the simplest dishes are the most satisfying. Once in a while, I like nothing better than these breaded chicken breasts—pan-fried in a combination of butter and olive oil, then baked in the oven. The lemon wedges are a new touch for my American customers, but the lemon lightens up the flavor of the fried breadcrumbs.

Serve this with *Spinaci* (page 154), *Melanzane alla Parmigiana* (page 156), or *Pomodori Reali* (page 160).

SERVES 4

1 cup/100g dried breadcrumbs

4 boneless chicken breast halves (from two 1-lb/450g breasts)

2 tablespoons olive oil

2 tablespoons unsalted butter

Fine sea salt

Freshly ground black pepper

1 lemon, cut into at least 4 wedges

Preheat the oven to 350°F/180°C/gas 4.

Spread the breadcrumbs out on a clean, dry surface and roll the chicken pieces in the crumbs, pressing down a bit to make sure they adhere.

Warm the olive oil and melt the butter in an ovenproof sauté pan large enough to hold all 4 breasts over medium heat. Add the breaded chicken and cook for 2 minutes on each side. As the chicken cooks, season the upward-facing side with salt and pepper.

Transfer the pan to the oven and cook until the chicken is cooked through, 7 to 10 minutes. Cut one open with a thin, sharp-bladed knife to check for doneness.

Remove the pan from the oven and transfer the chicken to a serving platter. If you like, you can cut the pieces crosswise into thin strips. Serve the lemon wedges alongside.

WINE SUGGESTION: **Dolcetto d'Alba–Marcarini**

POLLO ALLA BIRRA

CHICKEN COOKED IN BEER

Simmering chicken slowly in a light-style beer cooks it very gently and produces succulent results. If you've ever washed down roast chicken with a pint of beer, then you already know how well the flavors complement one another. In fact, that's how I got the idea for this recipe.

We used to serve *Pollo alla Birra* almost every day at Da Silvano, but I had to stop because the guys in the kitchen were drinking all the beer. Enjoy it at home with *Bietola* (page 166), boiled potatoes, or rice.

SERVES 4

1 chicken, preferably organic free range (3 to 4 lb/1.3 to 1.8kg), cut into 8 pieces

1¼ cups/170g all-purpose flour

Fine sea salt

Freshly ground black pepper

¼ cup/55ml olive oil

3 bottles light-style beer

Rinse the chicken pieces and pat dry with paper towels. Spread the flour out on a clean, dry surface and season it with salt and pepper. Press the chicken pieces into the flour.

In a large casserole, warm the olive oil over medium-high heat. Add the chicken pieces and brown on both sides, 3 to 4 minutes per side. Add the beer and raise the heat to high.

When the beer begins to boil, season it with salt and pepper. Stir the pot gently, lower the heat, and let simmer for 30 to 40 minutes. Use tongs to transfer the chicken to a platter and cover it to keep it warm.

Strain the sauce through a fine-mesh strainer. Spoon some sauce over the chicken and serve immediately.

WINE SUGGESTION: **Beer (maybe the 3 beers left over from the six-pack you bought to make this dish) or Dolcetto d'Alba–Marcarini**

faraona al barolo

GUINEA HEN COOKED IN BAROLO WINE

Full-bodied Barolo wines might overpower a chicken, but they are a perfect match with guinea hen. I use a three-step process to make this dish. First, I brown the hens in a sauté pan to get the skin nice and crispy. Then, I transfer it to the oven with porcini mushrooms to roast, which cooks the meat to succulent perfection. Finally, I return the hens to the stovetop and cook them in a small quantity of wine, to meld the flavors and create a wonderful pan sauce.

This is delicious with *Purè di Patate* (page 164) or fresh green beans.

SERVES 4

1 cup/30g dried porcini mushrooms

2 guinea hens (2½ to 3 lb/ 1.1 to 1.3kg each), necks and innards discarded and wings trimmed

2 cups/285g all-purpose flour

Fine sea salt

Freshly ground black pepper

4 tablespoons/55g (½ stick) unsalted butter

3 cups/675ml Barolo wine, or more as needed

Place the mushrooms in a stainless steel or ceramic bowl and cover with hot water. Let soak for 20 minutes or until reconstituted.

While the mushrooms are soaking, preheat the oven to 350°F/180°C/gas 4.

Rinse the hens under cold running water and pat them dry. Cut the hens in half lengthwise.

Spread the flour out on a clean, dry surface and season it with salt and pepper. Roll the hen halves in the seasoned flour to coat on both sides.

Melt 2 tablespoons butter in each of 2 ovenproof sauté pans over high heat. Add 1 hen, skin side down, to each pan and cook until browned on the bottom, 3 to 4 minutes. Flip the hens and cook until browned on the other side, 3 to 4 more minutes.

Drain and gently squeeze any excess water out of the porcini mushrooms and scatter them over the hens.

Place the sauté pans in the oven and cook until the hens are cooked through, 30 to 35 minutes. Remove them from the oven as soon as they are done; they will begin to fall apart if overcooked. Return the pans to the stovetop.

Pour half the wine over each hen and cook over medium heat for about 10 minutes. If the wine reduces completely, add a little more to the pan.

Remove the guinea hen halves from the pans and divide them among 4 dinner plates. Whisk the sauce in the pans, scraping up any bits that are stuck to the bottom. Spoon some sauce and mushrooms over each hen-half and serve immediately.

WINE SUGGESTION: **"Solaia"–Antinori**

quaglie alla griglia

Clean, fresh Cime di Rapa is a perfect side dish for this. If you serve it, mound some in the middle of the serving platter and place the quail on top of the broccoli.

serves 4

4 boneless quail (4 to 6 oz/
110 to 170g each)

4 sage leaves

2 tablespoons olive oil

Fine sea salt

Freshly ground black pepper

1 lemon, halved

Prepare an outdoor grill and let the coals burn until covered with white ash.

Rinse the quail and pat dry with paper towels. Place a sage leaf inside the cavity of each quail. Drizzle some olive oil over each quail and use your fingers to spread it evenly over the surface of the birds. Season with salt and pepper.

When the grill is ready, oil the grate. Place the quail on the grill and cook for 7 to 8 minutes on each side, turning only once.

Transfer the quail to a serving platter and finish with a squeeze of lemon. Serve immediately.

WINE SUGGESTION: **Cabernet–Cignale**

anatra al forno

VERTICALLY ROASTED DUCK

With duck, the most important thing is a crisp, crackling skin. This can be achieved by basting the duck with its own fat, which is accomplished here by using a vertical roaster, so the fat runs down the side of the bird as it cooks. The flavor of vermouth infuses the duck meat when it is cooked over the spirit, providing cool relief from its rich flavor.

You will need two vertical roasters for this recipe.

SERVES 4

2 Long Island ducks (about 7 lb/3.2kg each), liver and neck removed

Fine sea salt

Freshly ground black pepper

4 tablespoons unsalted butter

4 cups/900ml dry vermouth

Preheat the oven to 400°F/200°C/gas 6.

Rinse the ducks under cold water and pat dry with paper towels. Season them all over with salt and pepper. Place the ducks, legs side down, on the vertical roasters. Pour the vermouth into the bottom of an ovenproof casserole large enough to hold the ducks on their roasters, or divide it among 2 casseroles large enough to hold 1 roaster with its duck.

Stand the roasters in the casserole(s), balance 2 tablespoons butter on top of each duck, using the neck flap to keep the butter in place if possible, and transfer the casserole(s) to the oven. Cook for 30 minutes.

Reduce the heat to 325°F/170°C/gas 3 and cook for 3½ hours. Check periodically; if the ducks appear to be drying out, lower the heat to 300°F/150°C/gas 2. Remove the ducks from the casserole(s) and allow them to rest on their roasters for 2 minutes.

Halve the ducks lengthwise, transfer the pieces to a large serving platter, splash some hot vermouth over the pieces, and serve.

WINE SUGGESTION: **Pinot Noir–Marchesi Pancrazi**

CONIGLIO IN casseuROLa

It's sad how many people in the United States are unfamiliar with the pleasures of rabbit. The idea of butchering a rabbit intimidates many people but it's very easy, actually—certainly no more complicated than working with a chicken. For this recipe, you simply remove the front and hind legs and then use a cleaver to cut the saddle into four sections. You can also ask your butcher to do this for you, but if you do, be sure to ask him to reserve the liver and kidneys.

In this dish, the gamey flavor of rabbit is complemented by rosemary and sage for a very rustic effect. Serve it with *Purè di Patate* (page 164), which will soak up the delicious sauce or garnish it with *Foglie di Salvia Fritte* (page 35) to emphasize the sage flavor.

½ cup/110ml olive oil

1 rabbit, fryer size (about 3 lb/ 1.3kg), cut into 8 pieces (front legs, hind legs, and 4 saddle pieces), liver and kidneys chopped together and reserved

Fine sea salt

Freshly ground black pepper

1 sprig of rosemary, roughly chopped

8 sage leaves, roughly chopped

serves 4

Preheat the oven to 350°F/180°C/gas 4.

Warm 4 tablespoons of the olive oil in a pan large enough to hold the rabbit over medium heat. Add the rabbit pieces, season with salt and pepper, and cook, turning the pieces, until they are golden brown all over, about 8 minutes. Remove the pan from the heat and set aside.

Warm the remaining 4 tablespoons olive oil in an ovenproof casserole large enough to hold the rabbit pieces over medium heat. Add the reserved chopped rabbit liver and kidneys, the rosemary, sage, and garlic and cook until the garlic has colored slightly, about 2 minutes. Add the rabbit pieces. Cook, stirring, for 3 to 4 minutes.

Lean away from the casserole and add the Cognac, being careful not to let any Cognac spill over the side of the casserole because it can flare up on

3 garlic cloves, smashed and peeled

2 tablespoons Cognac

3 cups/675ml dry white wine

contact with the heat. Cook until the Cognac evaporates, about 1 minute. Add the wine, raise the heat to high, and bring to a boil.

Immediately cover the casserole and place it in the oven. Cook for 45 to 60 minutes, or until the rabbit pieces are done. As the rabbit cooks, check the casserole periodically to be sure the liquid is gently simmering; if it's boiling rapidly, lower the heat to 325°F/170°C/gas 3.

Remove the casserole from the oven, remove the rabbit pieces from the pan, and place them on a serving platter. Spoon some sauce over the rabbit and serve immediately.

WINE SUGGESTION: **Brunello–Fuligni**

Bistecca alla fiorentina

FLORENTINE STEAK

In Florence, we enjoy grilled porterhouse steak so much that a gigantic porterhouse grilled over hardwood coals today goes by the name *Bistecca alla Fiorentina*.

The porterhouse is the best short-loin cut of beef because it is made up of both the sirloin and the tenderloin and the bone delivers incredible flavor to the meat when cooked. For the best result, spend the extra money to buy prime, dry-aged steak as we do at Da Silvano. Dry-aged steaks are stored for several weeks in conditions that concentrate the flavor and tenderize the beef. Dry-aging makes a big difference, especially when there's no sauce to help the flavor.

Another thing about true Florentine steak—it should be enjoyed rare, rare, rare, so don't overcook it. One way to do this is to bank the coals to one side of the grill. If you feel the steak is getting too hot, cook the second side over the indirect heat on the side without the coals.

Serve this steak with *Purè di Patate* (page 164), *Cime di Rapa* (page 163), or, in the summer, *Pomodori Reali* (page 160)

SERVES 4

1 porterhouse (T-bone) steak, at least 2 inches/5 cm thick, preferably dry-aged (2½ to 3 lb/ 1.1 to 1.3kg)

Fine sea salt

Freshly ground black pepper

Extra virgin olive oil, for drizzling

1 lemon, quartered

Remove the steak from the refrigerator and let it rest at room temperature, covered with an inverted dinner plate, for about 30 minutes.

Prepare an outdoor grill, letting the coals burn down until covered with white ash.

Oil the grill grate, place the steak on the grill, and grill for 5 to 6 minutes on each side for rare or 7 to 9 minutes for medium. Season the upward-facing side with salt and pepper while the steak is on the grill. Do not move the steak while it is cooking; you want to produce dark grill marks. Remove the steak from the grill and let rest for 5 minutes so the juices can redistribute.

Cut the meat from the bone, then slice it into ¼ to ½-inch/0.5 to 1-cm slices. Arrange on a platter and drizzle with extra virgin olive oil. Squeeze the lemon over the slices, or pass the lemon wedges alongside.

WINE SUGGESTION: **Tignanello–Antinori or Brunello–Costanti**

BOLLito DI manzo

BOILED SHORT RIBS

This recipe may look very simple, but the flavors are actually very complex. By burning the onion over a gas flame before placing it in the poaching water, you give the meat a pleasing, smoky accent. The bones give the meat additional flavor, and the *Salsa Verde* livens up the dish.

Serve this with boiled vegetables of your choosing. You can cook them in a separate pot, or add them to the pot with the short ribs for the last 15 minutes of cooking time.

serves 4

1 medium red onion, peeled

Fine sea salt

Freshly ground black pepper

8 short ribs of beef (1¼ to 1½ lb/560 to 675g each)

1 large carrot, peeled and cut in half, or 2 small carrots, peeled

1 celery stalk, cut in half

1 cup/225g *Salsa Verde* (page 187)

Bring a stockpot full of water to a boil over high heat. While the water is heating up, burn the onion over a gas flame until it is dark brown or black all over, about 3 minutes on each side.

When the water reaches a boil, season it with salt and pepper. Carefully lower the short ribs, the onion, the carrot, and the celery into the pot. Boil the beef, skimming any fat or impurities that rise to the surface, until the ribs are cooked, about 1 hour 15 minutes. Remove the ribs from the water using tongs.

Transfer the ribs to a platter and serve with the *Salsa Verde* on the side.

WINE SUGGESTION: **Masseto–Ornellaia**

stracotto alla fiorentina

BRAISED BEEF, FLORENCE STYLE

When I think of winter cooking, one of the things that comes to mind is the long, slow braising that makes meat tender and flavorful. So it's no surprise that I love eating a *stracotto* (the name means "cooked for a very long time") in the dead of winter. Here, beef is cooked in a mixture of red wine, tomatoes, and mushrooms until it is fork-tender. When I was a child, this was one of the dishes my mother would often make for Sunday dinner.

Serve this with *Purè di Patate* (page 164) or *Spinaci* (page 154).

This recipe produces more sauce than you will need for the meat. The extra is delicious on top of polenta or tossed with pasta the next day.

serves 4

1 eye of the round roast, excess fat trimmed (2½ lb/1.1kg)

Fine sea salt

Freshly ground black pepper

4 ounces/110g salt pork, cut into small dice

2 medium red onions, peeled and quartered

1 large carrot, peeled and sliced into ¼-inch/0.5-cm rounds

4 celery stalks, cut crosswise into ¼-inch/0.5-cm rounds

Preheat the oven to 300°F/150°C/gas 2.

Season the beef with salt and pepper.

Warm the salt pork in an ovenproof casserole large enough to hold all the ingredients over medium-high heat. As soon as the pork gives off enough fat to coat the bottom of the casserole, add the beef and brown on all sides, about 4 minutes per side. (Tongs are a good tool to use to manipulate the meat.) Remove the beef and reserve.

Add the onions, carrot, and celery and cook, stirring gently, until the onions have colored slightly, about 7 minutes. Add the wine, raise the heat to high, and cook until the wine has reduced by half, about 5 minutes. Add

½ bottle (about 1¼ cups/385ml) dry red wine, or as needed

½ cup/30g dried porcini mushrooms, reconstituted in hot water and squeezed of excess liquid

1 can (28 oz/800g) high-quality plum tomatoes, drained of liquid

the mushrooms and tomatoes and season with salt and pepper, being mindful of the fact that the salt pork is salty.

Return the beef to the casserole. It should be half to three quarters covered by the liquid. If it is not, add more wine. Leave the casserole over high heat until the liquid returns to a boil. Cover the casserole and place it in the oven for 2½ to 3 hours. Every half-hour, turn the beef 180° and give the liquid a stir. When you do, make sure that the liquid is simmering gently; if it's bubbling aggressively, reduce the oven temperature to 275°F/140°C/gas 1.

Remove the casserole from the oven. Remove the beef and slice it into 6 to 8 pieces. Serve with sauce spooned over each serving and pass extra sauce on the side in a sauceboat.

WINE SUGGESTION: **Lupicaia–Tenuta del Terriccio**

OSSO BUCO aLLa miLanese

This isn't a Tuscan dish per se, but I grew to love it when I was in the Italian army, stationed in Bologna in 1966, right before the flood hit Florence. I was in charge of the mechanized infantry as a tank "pilot"—what a ball! (I actually first learned to drive an M47 tank when I was eleven years old, living in Florence as the army-brat son of a "Super Lieutenant.") The army was fun for me: I got to drive a tank all day, then go out and eat osso buco at night.

I still serve osso buco the classic way, with Risotto alla Milanese (page 74) underneath and gremolata on top.

Ask your butcher to cut the veal shanks three inches thick.

serves 4

Zest of 2 lemons

2 tablespoons roughly chopped flat-leaf parsley

1 cup/140g all-purpose flour

4 center-cut veal shanks, tied with kitchen string (12 oz to 1 lb/350 to 450g each)

Fine sea salt

Freshly ground black pepper

½ cup/110ml plus 2 tablespoons olive oil

2 celery stalks, roughly chopped

Preheat the oven to 350°F/180°C/gas 4.

To prepare the gremolata, place the lemon zest and parsley on the cutting board and roughly chop them together. Reserve.

To prepare the osso buco, spread the flour out on a clean, dry surface. Dredge the veal shanks in the flour to coat the top, bottom, and sides, then season them all over with salt and pepper. Heat 6 tablespoons of the olive oil in an ovenproof casserole large enough to hold all the ingredients over high heat. When the oil is hot, add the veal shanks and brown on all sides, 1 to 2 minutes per side. (Kitchen tongs are ideal for manipulating the shanks.) Remove the veal from the pan and reserve.

1 medium red onion, roughly chopped

½ large carrot or 1 small carrot, peeled and cut into ¼-inch/ 0.5-cm-thick rounds

4 cups/900ml white wine, or more as needed

1 bay leaf

In another pan, warm the remaining 4 tablespoons of olive oil over medium-high heat. When the oil is hot, add the celery, onion, and carrot. Cook, stirring, until the onion has colored slightly, about 7 minutes. Return the shanks to the casserole and pour the vegetables over them. Pour the white wine into the casserole and add the bay leaf. If the wine does not come almost to the top of the shanks, add enough to almost cover. Season with salt and pepper.

Place the casserole over high heat and bring the wine to a boil. Cover the casserole with a tight-fitting lid (or aluminum foil) and place in the oven. Cook until the shanks are fork-tender and warmed through, 2 to 2½ hours. Check the pot periodically to be sure the liquid is simmering very gently; if it's bubbling rapidly, lower the heat to 325°F/170°C/gas 3.

Remove the casserole from the oven, remove the osso buco from the casserole, and snip off and discard the kitchen string. Strain and degrease the sauce.

Serve hot, spooning some sauce over each portion and topping with the gremolata.

SUGGESTED WINE: **Campaccio Riserva–Terrabianca**

Stinco d'Agnello (Braised Lamb Shanks)

To make braised lamb shanks, simply replace the veal shanks with lamb shanks, and only use half a celery stalk; its sweetness doesn't marry well with the lamb.

viteLLo tonnato

Vitello Tonnato, in which cooked veal is cooled, then thinly sliced and layered with a sauce made by mixing canned tuna, mayonnaise, capers, and anchovies, is a quintessential Italian recipe. In the original, the veal and sauce are stacked, like a *lasagne*, and refrigerated overnight. I like the contrast between the freshly cooked veal and the sauce, so I serve it as soon as it's cooled.

When I think of *Vitello Tonnato*, I think of enjoying it outside in the spring or summer, so begin a meal that will feature it with seasonal accompaniments like *Fiori di Zucca* (page 159) or *Asparagi* (page 161).

serves 4

2 pounds/900g veal butt

Fine sea salt

Freshly ground black pepper

1 carrot, peeled and cut crosswise into ¼-inch/ 0.5-cm-thick rounds

1 small red onion, cut in half and then thinly sliced

1 celery stalk, cut crosswise into ¼-inch/0.5-cm-thick pieces

4 sage leaves

2 tablespoons capers, plus more for garnish, drained but not rinsed

2 cans (5½ oz/150g each) Italian tuna packed in oil

4 anchovy fillets, minced

1 cup/225g maionese (page 189)

2 large lemons, each cut into 8 slices

Preheat the oven to 325°F/170°C/gas 3.

Season the veal on all sides with salt and pepper and place in an ovenproof casserole. Scatter the carrot, onion, and celery over the veal and season them with salt and pepper.

Scatter the sage leaves over the vegetables. Place the casserole in the oven and roast until the veal is medium-rare, 1 hour to 1 hour 15 minutes, or until an instant-read thermometer inserted in the thickest portion of the veal reads 160°F/75°C. Remove the casserole from the oven and let the veal cool to room temperature.

To make the tuna sauce, place the capers, tuna, and anchovies in a blender and process until well incorporated. Pour the *maionese* into a mixing bowl. Add the caper-tuna-anchovy mixture and stir well. If the sauce seems too thick, add warm tap water while stirring to thin it until pourable.

Use a slicing knife or very sharp, thin-bladed knife to slice the veal paper-thin horizontally and divide the slices among 4 plates. Spoon the sauce over the veal until each portion is completely covered.

Garnish each plate by placing a few capers on top of the veal and 4 lemon slices at the edges of the plate. Serve immediately.

WINE SUGGESTION: **Picolit, "Rocca"–Bernarda**

PORCHetta

Sometimes if I am invited by a friend to the Hamptons for a weekend, I'll bring along a pig. This way I can roast the dinner, walk away from the kitchen, and enjoy the sea and sunshine. It tastes so good people think I was working over the stove all day.

serves at least 25

1 whole pig (15 to 18 lb/ 6.75 to 8kg)

8 garlic cloves, peeled

Fine sea salt

Freshly ground black pepper

2 cups/110g minced rosemary

Preheat the oven to 400°F/200°C/gas 6.

Rub the pig all over with the garlic. Season all over with salt, pepper, and rosemary. Sit the pig in a large roasting pan, bending it over so it will fit in the oven. Cover the pig's ears with foil. Place the roasting pan in the oven and cook for 45 minutes.

Lower the oven temperature to 275°F/140°C/gas 1 and cook for another 3 to 3½ hours, basting once after 2½ hours.

Remove the pig from the oven, let it rest for 30 minutes, then serve whole at the table or from a buffet.

WINE SUGGESTION: **Barbera d'Asti–Bricco dell'Uccellone**

PaiLLarD D'agNeLLo

Vogue editor Anna Wintour loves this dish "black and blue," meaning almost raw. Though I prefer it cooked on the grill, you can also make it indoors using a grill pan or cast-iron skillet. Serve it with *Melanzane alla Griglia* (page 155) or grilled vegetables of your choosing, such as tomatoes, asparagus, and peppers.

SERVES 4

8 slices lamb, cut horizontally from 2 top butts (about 2 lb/ 900g each)

12 tablespoons roughly chopped rosemary needles

12 tablespoons roughly chopped sage leaves

½ cup/110ml olive oil, plus more for oiling the grill grate

Fine sea salt

Freshly ground black pepper

1 lemon, halved

Prepare an outdoor grill, letting the coals burn down until covered with white ash.

Place each lamb slice between 2 sheets of plastic wrap and use a meat tenderizer or heavy-bottomed pan to pound it to a thickness of ¼ inch/0.5 cm.

Place the rosemary and sage in a bowl and stir together. Remove the lamb pieces from the plastic and sprinkle 3 tablespoons of the rosemary-sage marinade over each slice.

When the grill is ready, oil the grate.

Place the lamb slices on the grill. Cook for about 2 minutes on each side, seasoning the upward-facing side with salt and pepper as the lamb cooks. The meat should be rare.

Remove the lamb from the grill and arrange it on a platter. Allow it to rest about 1 minute. Drizzle 1 tablespoon olive oil and squeeze some lemon juice over each paillard.

WINE SUGGESTION: **Chianti Classico Riserva–Fonterutoli**

fegato DI VITELLO aLLa saLvia

CALF'S LIVER WITH SAGE

Calf's liver, or veal liver, is another delicious food that Americans are far too unfamiliar with. It's also one of the easiest things in the world to cook. The two keys are not to overcrowd the pan, which can cause the liver to become mushy, and not to overcook it, which can cause it to dry out.

Serve calf's liver with *Purè di Patate* (page 164).

SERVES 4

2 slices calf's livers, butterflied by your butcher (about ¼-inch/ 0.5-cm thick butterflied)

Fine sea salt

Freshly ground black pepper

8 sage leaves

2 tablespoons unsalted butter

Season the liver slices with salt and pepper. Place a sage leaf on each side of both liver slices.

Warm 2 pans, each large enough to hold 1 slice of liver, over medium heat, letting it get very hot. Place 1 tablespoon butter in each pan. When the butter starts to melt, add 1 liver slice to each pan. Cook for about 3 minutes on each side.

Remove the pans from the heat and allow the meat to rest for about 1 minute. Serve hot from a platter or on individual plates.

WINE SUGGESTION: **Sammarco–Castello di Rampolla**

insalata di trippa

My mother hates tripe: the sight of it, the smell of it cooking, the way it feels, but especially the taste. So as a child when I would go with my parents and sister to the old Mercato Centrale in Florence, the one destroyed in the terrible floods of 1966, my father and I would sneak off to have a bowl of tripe at a little restaurant in a nearby alley.

serves 4

2 pounds/900g honeycomb tripe

Fine sea salt

Freshly ground black pepper

1 celery stalk, cut into 1-inch/
2.5-cm pieces

1 large carrot, peeled and cut
into 1-inch/2.5-cm pieces

1 medium red onion, quartered
with roots left attached

1 sage leaf

1 medium red onion, roughly
chopped

2 plum tomatoes, roughly
chopped

Pinch of crushed red pepper

3 tablespoons minced flat-leaf
parsley

5 tablespoons olive oil

Splash of red wine vinegar

Splash of Tabasco sauce

Fill a large pot with water and bring it to a boil over high heat. When the water boils, season it with salt and pepper and add the celery, carrot, the quartered onion, and the sage. Add the tripe, lower the heat to let the liquid simmer, and cook until the tripe is tender, 2½ to 3 hours.

Drain the tripe, discard the cooking vegetables, and let it cool to room temperature. Slice the tripe into pieces ½ inch/1 cm wide and 3 inches/ 8 cm long.

Place the tripe slices in a mixing bowl. Add the chopped onion, the tomatoes, red pepper, and parsley. Drizzle with the olive oil and add a splash of red wine vinegar and a splash of Tabasco. Season with salt and pepper, toss well, and serve.

WINE SUGGESTION: **Pinot Bianco–Villa Russiz**

verdure

VEGETABLES

At Da Silvano, most of our main course dishes are presented unadorned and we give our customers the option of ordering a vegetable on the side, or not. This reinforces the homey quality of a meal at Da Silvano as side dishes are passed and shared among the people at the table, just as they might be in your family's dining room.

This chapter includes the most popular vegetable dishes from the Da Silvano menu. Many of them are quite basic, like my recipes for steamed spinach, sautéed *broccoli di rapa*, Swiss chard, mashed potatoes, sautéed zucchini, grilled eggplant, and *Pomodori Reali*, or royal tomatoes, in which slices of beefsteak tomato are covered with a salad of minced vegetables.

Cheese can make even simple vegetable preparations seem complex, and Parmigiano-Reggiano is used to great effect in three of

the recipes that follow. In *Melanzane Parmigiana*, browned slices of eggplant are layered with tomato sauce and cheese and baked in a casserole. In *Asparagi*, steamed asparagus is hidden under wide slices of cheese. And in *Finocchio Parmigiano*, braised fennel is topped with cheese that is browned just before serving.

I've also included the Tuscan classic *Fiori di Zucca Fritti*, or fried zucchini blossoms, which are delicious as an appetizer in the warm months of the year, and can also be used to garnish soups and risotto.

As you will have noticed in the previous chapters, I offer pairing suggestions for dishes that go well with these vegetable recipes, but you should feel free to let your own taste guide you as well, or to enjoy these recipes on their own for a light meal or snack.

spinaci

In my method for cooking spinach, you steam it and boil it at the same time. Be sure to force out as much water as possible before dressing it with the olive oil and lemon.

serves 4

Fine sea salt

Freshly ground black pepper

1 pound/450g fresh flat-leaf spinach, tough stems trimmed, and well washed in several changes of cold water

2 tablespoons olive oil

1 lemon, halved

Bring ½ inch/1 cm of water to a boil in a deep-sided pan large enough to hold the spinach and season it with salt and pepper. Add the spinach to the pan, cover, and cook for 3 minutes. Drain the spinach in a colander, pressing down on it with a wooden spoon to squeeze out as much water as possible.

Transfer the spinach to a serving bowl, season with salt and pepper, drizzle with olive oil, and squeeze the lemon over the spinach, using your hand to catch any seeds. Toss.

Serve immediately.

meLanzane aLLa griGLia

The char flavor created by a grill is the perfect complement to sweet, soft eggplant.

SERVES 4

4 small Italian eggplants
(2½-3 oz/70-85g each)

½ cup vegetable oil, plus more
to oil the grill grate

Fine sea salt

Freshly ground black pepper

2 tablespoons balsamic vinegar

Prepare an outdoor grill, letting the coals burn down until covered with white ash.

While the grill is heating up, slice the eggplants crosswise into ¼-inch/ 0.5-cm-thick slices. Brush the eggplant slices with the vegetable oil and season on both sides with salt and pepper. Oil the grill grate.

Place the eggplant on the grill. Grill for about 2 minutes on each side, seasoning the upward-facing side with salt and pepper.

Remove from the grill, drizzle with the balsamic vinegar, and serve.

meLanzane
parmigiana

EGGPLANT WITH PARMESAN CHEESE

You can make this dish with large eggplant, but I like the way the small ones provide bite-size pieces.

SERVES 4

4 small Italian eggplants
(2½ to 3 oz/70 to 85g each)

½ cup/55g all-purpose flour

Fine sea salt

Freshly ground black pepper

¾ to 1 cup/175 to 225ml olive oil

1 cup/225ml *Sugo di Pomodoro*
(page 182)

½ cup/55g freshly grated
Parmigiano-Reggiano

Preheat the oven to 400°F/200°C/gas 6.

Slice the eggplants crosswise into ¼-inch/0.5-cm-thick slices.

Season the flour with salt and pepper and spread it out on a clean, dry surface. Press the eggplant slices into the flour, coating them on both sides.

Warm 4 tablespoons of the olive oil in a wide sauté pan over medium heat. Add a third to half of the eggplant slices to the pan in a single layer and cook until they are golden brown on the bottom, about 3 minutes. Flip the slices and brown on the other side, 2 to 3 minutes. Remove to paper towels to drain. Repeat once or twice, adding 4 tablespoons of olive oil to the pan and heating it before each batch of eggplant, until all the eggplant slices have been browned and drained.

Pour 1 tablespoon olive oil into the bottom of a small ovenproof casserole and tilt and rotate the casserole to coat the bottom with the oil. Arrange a layer of eggplant on the bottom of the casserole. Cover with ¼ cup/55ml of the *sugo* and 2 tablespoons of the Parmigiano. Repeat twice with the remaining eggplant, sauce, and cheese, finishing with ½ cup/110ml tomato sauce and ¼ cup/30g Parmigiano.

Cover the casserole with foil and place it in the preheated oven. Bake for 15 minutes, then remove the foil and bake another 5 minutes to brown the Parmigiano.

Let rest for 5 minutes, then serve.

ZUCCHINI TRIFOLATI

SAUTÉED ZUCCHINI

When you purchase the zucchini for this recipe, make sure that it is firm and at the peak of freshness. You don't want it to get too mushy in the pan.

SERVES 4

4 very small zucchini (about 4 oz/110g each)

2 tablespoons olive oil

1 clove garlic, smashed and peeled

Fine sea salt

Freshly ground black pepper

6 tablespoons minced flat-leaf parsley

Cut off the ends of the zucchini and slice them into ¼-inch/0.5-cm-thick pieces. Warm the olive oil in a pan large enough to hold the zucchini over medium heat. Add the garlic and cook until lightly colored, about 2 minutes. Add the zucchini and season with salt and pepper. Sauté the zucchini, stirring occasionally, until lightly browned, 7 to 8 minutes.

Transfer to a platter and sprinkle with the parsley. Serve hot.

fiori di zucca fritti

Fried zucchini blossoms are a summertime ritual in Tuscany...and at Da Silvano.

SERVES 4

2 eggs, separated

2 cups/225g all-purpose flour

1 cup/225ml milk

1 cup/225ml light beer

Fine sea salt

Freshly ground black pepper

12 zucchini blossoms

1 cup/225ml vegetable oil

Whip the egg whites in a bowl until stiff peaks form.

In another large bowl, whisk together the flour, milk, egg yolks, and beer. Fold in the egg whites. Add the beer last while stirring the other ingredients. Add salt and pepper to taste. Coat each blossom with batter and set aside.

Warm the oil in a pan wide and deep enough to hold half of the blossoms over high heat. When the oil is hot but not smoking, add half of the blossoms to the pan and fry them until golden all over, about 3 minutes total cooking time.

Use tongs or a slotted spoon to transfer the blossoms to paper towels to drain.

Add more oil to the pan if necessary and fry the remaining blossoms in the same manner. Serve hot.

POMODORI REALI

ROYAL TOMATOES

This recipe is a perfect way to enjoy summer vegetables at the height of freshness. It takes only a minute to prepare, and is delicious and refreshing. Make it only when you have the highest quality ingredients because there's nothing for them to hide behind.

serves 4

4 big tomatoes, such as beefsteak tomatoes, trimmed and halved vertically

4 scallions, white parts only, roughly chopped

1 red pepper, stem, seeds and ribs removed and finely diced

1 green pepper, stem, seeds and ribs removed and finely diced

1 yellow pepper, stem, seeds and ribs removed and finely diced

½ medium red onion, finely diced

24 fresh basil leaves, torn into bite-size pieces

2 tablespoons olive oil

1 tablespoon red wine vinegar

Fine sea salt

Freshly ground black pepper

Arrange the tomato halves on a platter.

Put the scallions, red, yellow, and green peppers, onion, and basil in a bowl. Add the olive oil and vinegar, season with salt and pepper, and toss.

Pour the vegetable mixture over the tomatoes and serve.

asparagi

This is a very simple recipe, but asparagus, rucola, and Parmesan are a combination I had to include in this book.

serves 4

Fine sea salt

1 pound/450g large asparagus, trimmed and peeled

½ cup/30g chopped rucola

2 tablespoons Vinaigrette Modo Mio (page 186)

12 thin slices Parmigiano-Reggiano

Pour 2 inches/5 cm of water into a pot tall enough the hold the asparagus. Salt the water and bring it to a boil over high heat.

Stand the asparagus heads-up in a steamer compartment that will fit in the pot. Lower into the boiling water and cook for 9 to 10 minutes.

Drain the asparagus. Divide the stalks among 4 plates, top each with some rucola, drizzle with the vinaigrette, and then top each with 3 slices of Parmigiano-Reggiano.

cime di rapa

SAUTÉED BROCCOLI DI RAPA

Broccoli di rapa is a versatile Italian vegetable that goes very well with many poultry and meat dishes. The stems and leaves are edible, making for a very beautiful presentation at the table.

SERVES 4

2 pounds/900g broccoli di rapa, cut into 2 to 3-inch/5 to 7-cm pieces

3 tablespoons olive oil

4 cloves garlic, smashed and peeled

½ teaspoon crushed red pepper

Fine sea salt

Freshly ground black pepper

Warm the olive oil in a pan large enough to hold the broccoli di rapa over medium heat. Add the garlic and red pepper, season with salt and pepper, and cook until the garlic is slightly colored, about 2 minutes.

Add the broccoli di rapa, cover, and cook 3 to 7 minutes, depending on the thickness of the broccoli, removing the lid once or twice to stir.

Transfer the broccoli di rapa to a large serving bowl.

PURÈ DI patate

MASHED POTATOES

This is my recipe for mashed potatoes. They are especially good with poultry dishes but are also good with fish. If making mashed potatoes in advance, keep them warm in a double boiler set over low heat for up to two hours.

serves 4

Fine sea salt

2 pounds/900g Yukon Gold potatoes, scrubbed

1 cup/225ml milk

8 tablespoons (1 stick) unsalted butter, cut into 8 pieces

Freshly ground pepper, preferably white

Fill a pot large enough to hold the potatoes with salted water and bring it to a boil over high heat. Place the potatoes in the boiling water and cook for 20 to 30 minutes, or until tender. Test for doneness by inserting a sharp, thin-bladed knife into 1 potato. Drain the potatoes and allow to cool.

When the potatoes are cool enough to handle, remove the skins using a paring knife. Pass the potatoes through a ricer, or mash with a masher. Reserve the potatoes in a large, stainless steel bowl.

Pour the milk into a small pot and bring to a boil over high heat. As soon as it boils, carefully and gradually pour the milk over the potatoes, working them together with a wooden spoon as you add the milk. Add the butter, 1 piece at a time, stirring until it is incorporated and a thick purée is formed. Season with salt and pepper and stir again.

Transfer the purée to a serving bowl and serve immediately.

fINOCCHIO parmigiano

FENNEL WITH PARMESAN CHEESE

The anise flavor of fennel marries perfectly with sharp Parmesan cheese and dry white wine. If you like, chop up the fennel fronds and use them to garnish the finished dish.

serves 4

1 large fennel bulb (about 1 lb/450g)

2 tablespoons unsalted butter

2 tablespoons olive oil

½ cup/110ml dry white wine

½ cup/55g freshly grated Parmigiano-Reggiano

Preheat the oven to 350°F/180°C/gas 4.

Trim the fennel and cut it vertically into 6 to 8 thin slices. Set aside.

Melt the butter and warm the olive oil in a deep-sided sauté pan over medium heat. Add the fennel and season with salt and pepper. Cook for 2 minutes, then add the wine to the pan.

Cover and place the pan in the preheated oven. Cook until the fennel is just about al dente, about 20 minutes, depending on the freshness. Remove from the oven and sprinkle the cheese over the fennel.

Return the casserole to the oven and cook another 4 minutes, or until the cheese is melted. Serve hot.

Bietole

Swiss chard is less common than spinach, but it's often a better choice. It's a more sturdy green that pairs just as well with fish, poultry, and meat.

SERVES 4

4 tablespoons olive oil

2 cloves garlic, smashed, peeled, and roughly chopped

2 pounds/900g Swiss chard, tough stems removed

Fine sea salt

Freshly ground black pepper

Warm the olive oil in a pan large enough to hold the Swiss chard over medium heat. Add the garlic and cook until slightly colored, about 2 minutes. Add the Swiss chard, season with salt and pepper, and cook until wilted, 6 to 7 minutes. You might need to add the chard to the pan in batches.

Transfer to a serving bowl.

DOLCI

DESSERTS

Da Silvano doesn't specialize in desserts, but when people want something sweet to end the meal, it's important not to let them down. So, over the years, we've built a repertoire of reliable treats as traditional and satisfying as everything else on the menu.

A few of our desserts feature little twists that make them unique. For example, the Sgroppino replaces the traditional prosecco with vodka and the *Crema al Caramello* gets a lift from some lemon zest in the custard. One of our desserts has even become famous—the *Panna Cotta*. It's

firmer than most, and our customers absolutely love it. The *Crème Brulée* and *Torta di Formaggio* are fairly traditional but a bit richer than what you might be used to.

I think you'll like our desserts because they can be made ahead of time and kept, ready to go, in the refrigerator. That's how we do it in the restaurant, and I recommend you do the same at home to make your life a little easier...and sweeter.

SGROPPINO

LEMON SORBET BLENDED WITH VODKA

Sgroppino, a Venetian drink, is traditionally made by blending prosecco and lemon sorbet. But one night in Italy, a friend of mine introduced me to this version, made with vodka instead. I like it better, but you may want to warn your friends—it's got a big kick.

serves 4

1⅓ cups/225g lemon sorbet

1 cup/225ml premium vodka

Place 4 champagne flutes in the refrigerator to chill.

Put the sorbet and vodka in a blender. Blend on high speed until smooth. Pour into champagne glasses and serve immediately.

crema al caramello

This is our version of a crème caramel, with lemon zest in the custard to lighten up the rich cream and caramel flavors.

SERVES 6

1 pound/450g (2 cups) sugar

1 quart/1 litre milk

Finely grated zest of 1 lemon

8 egg yolks

3 teaspoons pure vanilla extract

Place 1 cup/225g of the sugar and ¼ cup/55ml of water in a nonreactive saucepan and cook over very low heat, stirring occasionally, until an amber caramel is formed, about 15 minutes. Ladle the caramel in a thin layer over the bottom of six 1-cup/225ml ramekins and allow to harden.

Place the milk and lemon zest in a small pot and bring to a boil over high heat. Immediately turn off the heat, or the milk will boil over.

Whisk the egg yolks with the remaining 1 cup/225g sugar and the vanilla. Slowly temper the hot liquid into the yolk mixture, whisking as you do. Divide the milk among the ramekins.

Place the ramekins in a baking pan and fill with warm water to about 1 inch/2.5 cm from the top of the ramekins.

Place the baking pan in the oven and bake until the custards firm up, 30 to 35 minutes.

Remove the pan from the oven, allow the custards to cool to room temperature, then remove the ramekins from the water and cover each one with plastic wrap. Refrigerate for at least 1 hour or up to 24 hours.

When ready to serve, remove the plastic wrap and run a small knife along the edge of each custard. Place a plate over each ramekin, invert, gently tap, and remove the ramekin, unmolding the custard onto the plate. Serve at once.

panna cotta

Traditionally *panna cotta* **is described as wobbly**—if you poke it with a fork it should practically collapse. But I believe that a *panna cotta* should be true to its name, which means *cooked* cream. So, while most people only boil the cream on the stovetop, I cook it in the oven until it really firms up. Trust me, this will be like no other *panna cotta* you've ever tasted.

serves 6

1 quart/1 litre heavy cream

2 tablespoons pure vanilla extract

½ cup/112.5g sugar

2 tablespoons unflavored powdered gelatin

½ cup/110ml high-quality chocolate sauce

Preheat the oven to 375°F/190°C/gas 5.

Whisk together the cream, vanilla, sugar, and gelatin in a small ceramic or stainless steel bowl. Transfer the mixture to a pot and set over high heat. Cook, stirring vigorously, until the mixture boils. Immediately remove from heat and divide the mixture among six 1-cup/225ml, ovenproof ramekins. Place the ramekins in a baking pan and fill the pan to a level of 1 inch/2.5 cm with cold water.

Place the pan in the oven and bake just until the liquid begins to thicken, about 10 minutes.

Remove the pan from the oven, remove the ramekins from the pan, cover each with plastic wrap, and transfer to the refrigerator. (This must be done immediately or the cream will separate. Work using tongs or oven mitts to protect your hands; the ramekins and cream will be hot.) Refrigerate for at least 3 hours or up to 24 hours.

When ready to serve, use a knife to gently release each *panna cotta* from its ramekin. Invert each one onto a plate, drizzle with chocolate sauce, and serve.

crème BruLée

At Da Silvano, we brand the restaurant's initials into the top of each crème. Obviously, you can't do this at home, but you should not skip the step of browning the sugar on top of each dessert—it's easy to do and the contrast between the cool custard and hot, crisp sugar is divine.

SERVES 6

12 egg yolks

3 cups/700ml heavy cream

1 cup/225ml whole milk

1 cup/225g granulated sugar

2 tablespoons pure vanilla extract

¼ cup/55g superfine sugar

Preheat the oven to 325°F/170°C/gas 3.

Whisk together all the ingredients in a ceramic or stainless steel mixing bowl. Divide the mixture among six 1-cup/225ml ovenproof ramekins. Place the ramekins in a baking pan and fill the pan with warm water up to 1 inch/2.5 cm from the tops of the ramekins.

Place the pan in the oven and bake until the custards are set but still a bit loose in the middle, about 35 to 40 minutes.

Remove the pan from the oven, remove the ramekins from the pan, and let the custard cool to room temperature. Cover each with plastic wrap, transfer to the refrigerator, and refrigerate for at least 3 hours or up to 24 hours.

When ready to serve, preheat the broiler.

Remove the plastic covering from each ramekin. Sprinkle a layer of superfine sugar over the surface of each one. Set the ramekins in a baking pan and fill with ice water almost to the tops of the ramekins. Place the pan under the broiler and bake until the sugar crystallizes, about 30 seconds. If you have a small propane torch, you can also caramelize the sugar using the torch.

Remove the ramekins from the pan, dry them off, and serve immediately.

torta di formaggio

This is not a New York cheesecake—it's much lighter and more crumbly. It's especially delicious with fresh berries.

makes one 12-inch cake

5 eggs, separated

5 tablespoons sugar

3 ounces/85g (about ⅜ cup) all-purpose flour

1 tablespoon pure vanilla extract

8 ounces/225g cream cheese, softened at room temperature

8 ounces/225g sour cream

8 ounces/225g buffala ricotta cheese

Butter, for greasing pan

Powdered sugar, for sprinkling

Preheat oven to 300°F/150°C/gas 2.

Whisk the egg yolks in a ceramic or stainless steel bowl, then whisk in the sugar, flour, and vanilla. Reserve.

In another bowl, use a rubber spatula to combine the cream cheese, ricotta cheese, and sour cream. Reserve.

In a third bowl, whip the egg whites until stiff peaks form. Fold the whites into the cheese-sour cream mixture, then gently fold in the egg yolk mixture. Work the mixture until it is well incorporated, but do so as gently as possible.

Lightly grease the bottom of a 12-inch/30-cm springform pan with butter. Pour the mixture into the pan, leaving at least 1 inch/2.5 cm of room at the top.

Bake until the top puffs up a bit and starts to color, 1 hour to 1 hour 15 minutes. To test for doneness, insert a toothpick into the center of the cake. It should come out clean.

Remove the pan from the oven and let cool to room temperature. Cover with plastic wrap and refrigerate for at least 1 hour or up to 24 hours.

When ready to serve, remove the cake from the springform pan, transfer to a platter or cake stand, and sprinkle with powdered sugar.

yummy yummy!
♡

BRODI e SUGHI

STOCKS AND SAUCES

SUGO DI POMODORO

This is the basic tomato sauce that we use in other recipes at Da Silvano, and throughout the book. If you want to make enough for a big group, or keep some extra in the freezer, the recipe multiplies very well.

makes about 2½ cups/560g

¼ cup/55ml olive oil

4 cloves garlic, smashed and peeled

6 tablespoons fresh basil leaves (loosely packed)

2 cups/450g plum tomatoes, peeled and roughly chopped, or 1 can (28 oz/800g) peeled plum tomatoes from Italy, in their juice, crushed by hand

Fine sea salt

Freshly ground black pepper

Warm the olive oil in a pot large enough to hold all the ingredients over medium heat. Add 2 cloves of the garlic and cook until lightly browned, about 3 minutes. Remove and discard the cloves using tongs or a slotted spoon.

Remove the pot from the heat and toss in the basil leaves and the remaining 2 cloves of garlic. Add the tomatoes and return the pot to the heat. Season with salt and pepper and stir. Cook over low heat for about 15 minutes.

Use the sauce right away or let it cool and store it in an airtight container in the refrigerator for up to 3 days or freeze for up to 2 months.

BRODO DI CARNE

BEEF STOCK

Use this stock in sauces, soups, and stews featuring beef or that call for a strong-flavored base.

makes about 4 quarts/4 litres

4 pounds/1.8kg beef bones

3 celery stalks, each cut into 3 large pieces

1 large carrot, peeled and cut into 3 large pieces

1 large red onion, peeled and quartered

20 sprigs of flat-leaf parsley

1 tablespoon fine sea salt

1 tablespoon black peppercorns

Preheat the oven to 350°F/180°C/gas 4.

Spread the beef bones out on a baking sheet and roast in the preheated oven for about 30 minutes. Remove and reserve.

Place all the ingredients in a stockpot. Add 4 quarts/4 litres of water and bring to a simmer over medium heat. Lower the heat to let the liquid simmer and continue to simmer for 3 to 4 hours, periodically skimming any impurities that rise to the surface.

Strain the stock through a fine-mesh strainer, allow to cool, and skim any fat that rises to the surface. Transfer to an airtight container and refrigerate for up to 3 days or freeze for up to 2 months. If freezing, divide the stock among smaller containers so that you defrost only as much as you need at any one time.

BRODO DI POLLO

Use this stock in sauces, soups, and stews featuring chicken or that call for a white stock.

makes about 4 quarts/4 litres

6 pounds/2.7kg chicken bones

3 celery stalks, cut into 3 large pieces

1 large carrot, peeled and cut into 3 large pieces

1 large red onion, peeled and quartered

20 sprigs of flat-leaf parsley

1 tablespoon fine sea salt

1 tablespoon black peppercorns

Place all the ingredients in a stockpot. Add 4 quarts/4 litres of water and bring to a simmer over medium heat. Lower the heat to let the liquid simmer and continue to simmer for 3 to 4 hours, periodically skimming any impurities that rise to the surface.

Strain the stock through a fine-mesh strainer, allow to cool, and skim any fat that rises to the surface. Transfer to an airtight container, and refrigerate for up to 3 days or freeze for up to 2 months. If freezing, divide the stock among smaller containers so that you defrost only as much as you need at any one time.

BRODO DI VERDURE

VEGETABLE STOCK

Use this stock to make vegetarian dishes or seafood dishes, like Risotto con Vongole (page 72), where you don't want the flavor of beef or chicken.

makes about 4 quarts/4 litres

2 celery stalks, each cut into
3 large pieces

1 medium red onion, quartered

2 cloves garlic, smashed and
peeled

1 tomato, halved, seeds squeezed
out and discarded

1 medium leek, white part only,
well washed and quartered

20 sprigs of flat-leaf parsley

1 tablespoon fine sea salt

1 tablespoon black peppercorns

Place all the ingredients in a stockpot. Add 4 quarts/4 litres of water and bring to a boil over high heat. Lower the heat to let the liquid simmer, and continue to simmer for 3 to 4 hours.

Strain the stock through a fine-mesh strainer. Allow to cool, transfer to an airtight container, and refrigerate for up to 3 days or freeze for up to 2 months. If freezing, divide the stock among smaller containers so that you defrost only as much as you need at any one time.

VINAIGRETTE MODO MIO

VINAIGRETTE MY WAY

This is a delicious, all-purpose salad dressing. The key is the soybean oil (a.k.a. vegetable oil), which is much lighter than olive oil.

¼ cup/55ml red wine vinegar
1¾ cups/400ml soybean oil
1 small garlic clove, minced
Pinch fine sea salt
Pinch freshly ground black pepper
Pinch dry mustard, preferably Colman's English Mustard

makes about 2 cups/½ litre

Place all the ingredients in a ceramic or stainless steel bowl. Whisk together well. Use right away or refrigerate in an airtight container for up to 3 days.

salsa verde

Many regions of Italy have their own version of *salsa verde,* or green sauce. This one has lots of bite.

makes about 3 cups/675g

4 cups/225g (loosely packed) flat-leaf parsley leaves, minced

1 cup/110g cornichons, roughly chopped

Pinch of crushed red pepper

2 anchovy fillets

¾ cup/170ml olive oil

Splash of red wine vinegar, if necessary

Juice of 1 lemon

Place the parsley, cornichons, red pepper, and anchovy fillets in a food processor and process until the ingredients are well blended. With the motor still running, add the olive oil in a thin stream. Continue to process until a thick paste is formed.

Transfer the *salsa verde* to a ceramic or stainless steel mixing bowl. Taste. If it doesn't have any bite, add a splash of red wine vinegar and stir. Add about half the lemon juice and stir. Taste and continue to add lemon juice a little at a time until the sauce is vibrant but not too acidic.

This sauce can be kept in an airtight container in the refrigerator for up to 3 days.

pesto

A lot of people romanticize pesto and think about tossing it in the pan with freshly cooked pasta. But you should never do that—it will turn the basil in the pesto black. Always mix pesto with hot pasta in a bowl.

Because I use pesto with a salmon recipe in the book (see page 96), I separate the cheese out in this recipe. That way, you can add the cheese only if you want or need it for a given purpose.

4 cups/225g (tightly packed) basil leaves

1 cup/140g pine nuts

1 clove garlic, smashed and peeled

1 cup/225ml olive oil

Fine sea salt

Freshly ground black pepper

About ½ cup/55g freshly grated Parmigiano-Reggiano

makes about 1 cup/225g

Place the basil, pine nuts, and garlic in a food processor. With the motor running, add the olive oil in a thin stream, then season with salt and pepper. Continue to process until a pourable liquid is formed.

Keep pesto in an airtight container in the refrigerator for up to 1 week. Pour a little film of olive oil over it to keep it as fresh as possible.

Add the cheese (about 1 tablespoon per person) just before serving or using.

maionese

Homemade mayonnaise tastes nothing like store-bought mayonnaise—it's far superior—and it's very easy to make.

makes about 1 cup/225g

1 large egg yolk

1 cup/225ml vegetable oil, such as soybean or canola

1 teaspoon dry mustard, preferably Colman's English Mustard

1 teaspoon Worcestershire sauce

Juice of ½ lemon, if necessary

Fine sea salt

Freshly ground black pepper

1 teaspoon red wine vinegar

Whisk the egg yolk in a ceramic or stainless steel bowl large enough to hold the oil. Gradually add the oil to the bowl in a thin stream, whisking to form a thick, emulsified mixture. When the mayonnaise has formed, whisk in the mustard and Worcestershire. Taste. If the mayonnaise seems too rich or unctuous, add a little of the lemon juice. Season with salt and pepper to taste.

Pour the red wine vinegar into a small pan and place over low heat just until slightly warm, about 30 seconds. Whisk the warm vinegar into the mayonnaise.

This mayonnaise should be used immediately.

panata

This is a versatile coating for fish and shellfish that's headed for the grill.

½ cup/55g dried breadcrumbs

½ teaspoon minced garlic

6 tablespoons minced flat-leaf parsley

¼ teaspoon crushed red pepper

makes about 1 cup/225g

Place all the ingredients on a cutting board and chop together until thoroughly incorporated. The garlic should be absorbed by the breadcrumbs and the parsley, pepper flakes, and crumbs should be indistinguishable from one another.

This can be stored in an airtight container in the refrigerator for up to 3 days.

mail-order sources

If you have trouble finding any of the ingredients or equipment in the recipes in this book, these world-class purveyors will ship to you, wherever you may be.

DEAN & DELUCA
www.deandeluca.com
800-221-7714
This gourmet market is an institution in New York City. They carry many hard-to-find meats, poultry, game, and cheeses, as well as every ingredient you could want, including high-quality olive oils.

CITARELLA
www.citarella.com
212-874-0383
Best-known for its fish and shellfish, this company also sells dry-aged meats as well as caviar and cheese.

D'ARTAGNAN
www.dartagnan.com
800-DARTAGN
In my opinion, the best supplier of game and foie gras.

URBANI TRUFFLES USA
www.urbani.com
800-281-2330
The best purveyor of truffles and wild mushrooms.

WILLIAMS-SONOMA
www.williams-sonoma.com
800-541-2233
This national chain sells cooking equipment, including slicing machines, ramekins, vertical roasters, and other items called for throughout the book.

guide to culinary terms

INGREDIENTS

all-purpose flour	plain flour
beets	beetroots
bibb lettuce	little gem lettuce
broccoli di rapa	sprouting broccoli
crushed red pepper	chili flakes
diver scallops	sea scallops
eggplant	aubergine
eye round of beef	topside of beef
fava beans	broad beans
fine sugar	caster sugar
guinea hen	guinea fowl
heavy cream	double cream
Idaho potatoes	baking potatoes
lamb top butt slices	boneless lamb shanks
Long Island duck	Pekin duck
raisins	sultanas
red pepper	chili
rucola	rocket
scallions	spring onions
short ribs of veal	veal chops
shrimp	prawns
veal butt	boned rolled veal
veal scallopine	veal escalopes
whole milk	full cream milk
zucchini	courgette

EQUIPMENT

broiler	grill
cookie sheet	baking tray
grate	rack
grill grate	barbecue rack
plastic wrap	clingfilm
stovetop	hob

INDEX